The Soul of the

Sketches from the Western Battle-Front

Thomas Tiplady

Alpha Editions

This edition published in 2024

ISBN : 9789357960953

Design and Setting By
Alpha Editions
www.alphaedis.com
Email - info@alphaedis.com

Contents

THE MOTHER'S ANSWER

God gave my son in trust to me.
Christ died for him. He should be
A man for Christ. He is his own
And God's and man's, not mine alone.
He was not mine to give. He gave
Himself, that he might help to save
All that a Christian should revere
All that enlightened men hold dear.

"To feed the guns." Ah! torpid soul,
Awake, and see life as a whole.
When freedom, honor, justice, right,
Were threatened by the despot's might,
He bravely went for God, to fight
Against base savages, whose pride
The laws of God and man defied;
Who slew the mother and the child;
Who maidens, pure and sweet, defiled;
He did not go to feed the guns,
He went to save from ruthless Huns
His home and country, and to be
A guardian of democracy.

"What if he does not come?" you say;

Well, then, my sky will be more gray,

But through the clouds the sun will shine

And vital memories be mine.

God's test of manhood is, I know

Not, will he come--*but did he go?*

JAMES L. HUGHES.

PREFACE

The sketches in this book and in my previous one, "The Cross at the Front," are attempts to show the soul of the soldier serving in France as I have seen it during the year and a half that I have been with him. It is a padre's privilege and duty to be the voice with which, in public worship, the soldiers speak to God; and through which their last thoughts are borne to their friends at home. He is their voice both when they are sick or wounded, and when they lie silent in the grave. He speaks of their hopes and fears, hardships and heroisms, laughter and tears. As best he may he tries to tell, to those who have a right and a longing to know, how they thought, and how they bore themselves in the great day of trial when all risked their lives and many laid them down.

Soldiers, as a rule, are either inarticulate or do not care to speak of themselves; and the padre has to be their spokesman if ever their deeper thoughts and finer actions are to be known to their friends. To do this he may have to bring himself into the picture, or even illustrate a common thing in their lives by a personal experience of his own. To reveal life and thought at the Front in the third person, and without sacrificing truth and vividness, requires a degree of literary power and art which cannot be expected of a padre to whom writing is but a by-product, and not his main work.

I have written but little of military operations--these things are not in my province. Moreover, they are not the things which are most revealing. The presence of Spring is first and most surely revealed by the flowers in our gardens and lanes; and the soldier is most clearly seen in the little things that happen on the march--in his billet or in the Dressing Station. Some things are not seen at all. They are only felt, and my opinion about them must be taken for what it is worth. One knows what the men are by their influence on one's own mind and life. I do not judge the morality and spirituality of our soldiers entirely by their habits and speech, for these are but outward and clumsy expressions of the inner life and are largely conventional. There is something else to put in the reckoning, and to find out what the soldiers are worth to us we must somehow get behind their words and actions and find out what they are worth to God, whose terrible wheel of war is shaping their characters.

I appraise them mostly by the total effect of the impact of their souls on mine. I know their thoughts and feelings by the thoughts and feelings they inspire in me. "Do men gather grapes of thorns or figs of thistles?" There are certain thoughts and emotions that only come to me strongly when I am with the soldiers or when I am living again with them in memory, and so, I take these as their gift to me and judge the men by their influence on my character. Character is, in its influence, subtle as Spring. Words and actions by themselves are too coarse and conventional to do anything but mislead us in judging the quality of our men. "By their fruits ye shall know them." Not by their leaves. Fruit is *seed*. In the seed the tree reproduces itself. And reproduction, whether in physical, moral or spiritual life, is the test of vitality.

I have not unduly loaded my pages with ghastly details of war, because their effect on the mind of the reader who has not been at the Front would be false and distorting. The reader would be more horrified in imagining them than our soldiers are in seeing them. I have tried rather to show life at the Front, with its mingling of red and gold, horror and happiness, as it affects the soldier; so that his friends at home may see it as he sees it, and with his sense of proportion. If I could only do it, as well as I intend it, my pictures would create a truer sympathy between the home and the trench. Some would find comfort for their hearts, and others would awake to a new and noble seriousness. Soldiers have suffered much through imperfect sympathies. They have been pitied for the wrong things, and left to freeze when they needed warmth. Only when we realize their dignity and greatness and the true nature of their experiences can we be their comrades and helpers. Life at the Front is brutal and terrifying, and yet our soldiers are neither brutalized nor terrorized, for there is something great and noble at the Front which keeps life pure and sweet and the men gentle and chivalrous. When "the boys" come home their friends will, in almost every case, find them just as bright, affectionate and good as when they went out. The only change will be a subtle one--a deepening in character and manly quality, a broadening in mind and creed, and an impatience with cant and make-believe whether in politics or business, Christianity or Rationalism. There will be an air of indefinable greatness about them as of men who have been at grips with the realities of life and death.

In a footnote to one of his songs, Edward Teschemacher says that the gypsies, as they wander through the country, leave a sprinkling of grass or wild flowers at the cross-roads to indicate, to those who come after them, the road they have taken. These flowers are known as the "Patterain."

These essays are my Patterain--wild flowers plucked in France, and left to mark the red path trod during the months I have been with my comrades at the Front.

I would the flowers were worthier, but such as I have, I give; and they are taken out of my heart.

"Where my caravan has rested

Flowers I leave you on the grass;

All the flowers of love and memory;

You will find them when you pass."

THOMAS TIPLADY.

I
THE SWAN AT YPRES

For three years the storm center of the British battle front has been at Ypres. Every day and night it has been the standing target of thousands of guns. Yet, amid all the havoc and thunder of the artillery, the graceful white form of a swan had been seen gliding over the water of the moat. It never lacked food, and was always welcome to a share of Tommy's rations. In the Battle of Messines--I had the story first-hand from a lieutenant of artillery whose battery was hidden close by, and who was an eye-witness of the incident--a shell burst near the swan, and it was mortally wounded. For three long years it had spread its white wings as gallantly as the white sails of Drake's flagship when he sailed out of Plymouth Sound to pluck the beard of the Spaniard. But now its adventurous voyaging was over. Another beautiful and innocent thing had been destroyed by the war and had passed beyond recall. There was no dying swan-song heard on the waters, but all who saw its passing felt that the war had taken on a deeper shade of tragedy.

Many a "white man" had been slain near the spot but somehow the swan seemed a mystical being, and invulnerable. It was a relic of the days of peace, and a sign of the survival of purity and grace amid the horrors and cruelties of war. It spoke of the sacred things that yet remain--the beautiful things of the soul upon which war can lay no defiling finger. Now it had gone from the water and Ypres seems more charred than ever, and the war more terrible. The death of the swan revealed against its white wings the peculiar inhumanity of the present war. It is a war in which the enemy spares nothing and no one. He is more blind and merciless than the Angel of Death which swept over Egypt, for the angel had regard to the blood which the Israelites had sprinkled over the lintels of their doors and he passed by in mercy. To the German Eagle every living creature is legitimate prey. No blood upon the lintel can save the inmate; not even the cross of blood on the hospital tent or ship. Wounded or whole, combatant or non-combatant, its beak and talons tear the tender flesh of all and its lust is not sated.

In Belgium and Serbia it is believed that more women and children perished than men. Things too hideous for words were done publicly in the market-squares. Neither age nor sex escaped fire and sword. The innocent babe was left to suck the breast of its dead mother or was dandled on the point of the bayonet. What resistance can the Belgian swan make to the German eagle? It needs must lie torn and bleeding beneath its talons. The German Emperor has waded deeper in blood than Macbeth, and has slain the innocent in their sleep. Even the sea is full of the women, children, and non-combatant men he has drowned. His crown is cemented together with innocent blood and its jewels are the eyes of murdered men and women. The wretched man has made rivers of blood to flow yet not a drop in them is from his own veins or the veins of his many sons. Napoleon risked his life with his men in every battle but this man never once. While sending millions to their death he yet consents to live, and protects his life with the anxious care a miser bestows on his gold. Alone among large families in Germany his household is without a casualty. Though a nation be white and innocent as the Belgian swan it will not escape his sword, and he will swoop upon it the more readily because it is unarmed. The swan cannot live where the eagle flies, and one or the other must die.

But the stricken swan of Ypres is not merely the symbol of Belgium and her fate. There are other innocents who have perished or been sorely wounded. The whole creation is groaning and travailing in pain. The neutral nations are suffering with the belligerent, and the lower creatures are suffering with mankind.

Next to seeing wounded men on the roads at the front, I think the saddest sight is that of dying horses and mules. Last winter they had to stand, with little cover, exposed to the bitter blasts. It was impossible to keep them clean or dry, for the roads were churned into liquid mud and both mules and drivers were plastered with it from head to foot. To make things worse there was a shortage of fodder; and horses waste away rapidly under ill-feeding. Before the fine weather had given them a chance to recover weight and strength, the Battle of Arras began, and every living beast of burden, as well as every motor-engine, was strained to its utmost. The mule is magnificent for war, and our battles have been won as much by mules as men. Haig could rely on one as much as on the other. The mule will eat anything, endure anything, and, when understood and humored by its driver, will do anything. It works until it falls dead by the roadside. In the spring, hundreds died in harness. In fact, few die except in harness. They die facing the foe, dragging rations along shell-swept roads to the men in the trenches.

On two miles of road I have counted a dozen dead mules; and burial parties are sent out to put them out of sight. One night, alone, I got three dying mules shot. The road was crowded with traffic, yet it was difficult to find either an officer with a revolver or a transport-driver with a rifle. I had to approach scores before I could find a man who had the means to put a mule out of its misery; and we were within two miles of our Front. So rigid is our line of defense that those behind it do not trouble to take arms. Even when I found a rifleman he hesitated to shoot a mule. There is a rule that no horse or mule must be shot without proper authority, and when you consider the enormous cost of one the necessity for the rule is obvious. I had therefore to assure a rifleman that I would take full responsibility for his action. He then loaded up, put the nozzle against the mule's forehead and pulled the trigger. A tremor passed through the poor thing's body and its troubles were over. It had come all the way from South America to wear itself out carrying food to fighting men, and it died by the road when its last ounce of strength was spent.

The mule knows neither love nor offspring. Apart from a few gambols in the field, or while tethered to the horse-lines, it knows nothing but work. It is the supreme type of the drudge. It is one of the greatest factors in the war, and yet it receives scarcely any recognition and more of whipping than of praise. Only too often I have seen their poor shell-mangled bodies lying by the roadside waiting till the battle allowed time for their burial. Yet what could be more innocent of any responsibility for the war? They are as innocent as the swan on the moat at Ypres.

Yet the greatest suffering among innocents is not found at the Front at all. It is found at home. At the Front there is suffering of body and mind, but at home there is the suffering of the heart. Every soldier knows that his mother and wife suffer more than he does, and he pities them from his soul. War is a cross on which Woman is crucified. The soldier dies of his wounds in the morning of life, but his wife lingers on in pain through the long garish day until the evening shadows fall. There is no laughter at home such as you hear at the Front, or even in the hospitals. One finds a gayety among the regiments in France such as is unknown among the people left at home. It is the sunshine of the street as compared with the light in a shaded room. There is a youth and buoyancy at the Front that one misses sadly in the homeland.

To a true woman with a son or husband at the Front, life becomes a nightmare. To her distorted imagination the most important man in the country is not the Prime Minister but the postman. She cannot get on with her breakfast for listening for his footsteps. There is no need for him to knock at the door, she has heard him open the gate and walk up the gravel path. Her heart is tossed like a bubble on the winds of hope and fear. She finds herself behind the door without knowing how she got there, and her hand trembles as she picks up the letter to see if the address is in "his" handwriting or an official's. The words, "On His Majesty's Service," she dreads like a witch's incantation. They may be innocent enough, and cover nothing more than belated Commission Papers, but she trembles lest they should be but the fair face of a dark-hearted messenger, who is to blot out the light of her life forever. If she goes out shopping and sees a telegraph-boy go in the direction of her home she forgets her purchases and hurries back to see if he is going to knock at her door. The rosy-faced messenger has become a sinister figure, an imp from the nether world. He may be bringing news of her loved one's arrival "on leave," but so many evil faces of fear and doubt peer through the windows of her heart that she cannot believe in the innocence and good-will of the whistling boy. Her whole world is wrapped up in his little orange-colored envelope.

The boys at the Front know of the anxiety and suspense that darken their homes, and they do all they can to lighten them. There were times on the Somme when the men were utterly exhausted with fighting and long vigils in the trenches. Water was scarce, and a mild dysentery came into evidence. No fire could be lighted to cook food or make hot tea. The ranks had been thinned, and only two officers were left to each company. The weather was bad and the captured trench uncomfortable. Any moment word might come for another attack. The campaign was near its close, and the work must be completed despite the prevalent exhaustion. The officers were too tired, depressed and preoccupied to censor hundreds of letters. In front of him each could see a gaping grave. The sun was rapidly "going west" and leaving them to the cold and dark. Nothing seemed to matter in comparison with *that*. To hold services were impossible and I felt that the best I could do was to walk through the trench, chat with the officers and men, gather up the men's letters and take them back and censor in my tent. This gave the officers times to write their own, and an opportunity to post them.

But note, I pray you, the nobility of these gallant fellows. All of them were exhausted and depressed. The shadows of death were thick about them, yet when I opened their letters, I found myself--with two exceptions out of three or four hundred--in an entirely different atmosphere. It was a sunny atmosphere in which birds were singing. The men said nothing of their suffering, their depression, their fears for the future. The black wings of death cast no shadow over their pages. They said they were "all right," "merry and bright" and "soon going back for a long rest." They told their mothers what kind of cigarettes to send, and gave them details how to make up the next parcel. They talked as if death were out of sight--a sinister fellow with whom they had nothing to do.

The officers, of course, censor their own letters, so I did not see how they wrote. But I know. They wrote as the men wrote, and probably with a still lighter touch. Their homes were dark enough with anxiety, yet not by any word of theirs would the shadows be deepened. They could not shield themselves from war's horrors but they would do their best to shield their white swans at home. They could not keep their women folk out of the war, but they would deliver them from its worst horrors. Not till they had fallen would they let the shafts pass them to their mothers and wives; rather would they gather them in their own breasts. In the hour of the world's supreme tragedy there was a woman standing by the cross, and the august Sufferer, with dying breath, bade His closest friend take her, when the last beam faded, to his own home and be in His place, a son to her. I know no scene that better represents the feelings of our soldiers towards their loved ones at home.

Their women gave them inspiration and joy in the days of peace, and they still float before their vision amid the blackened ruins of war, as beautiful and stainless in their purity as the white swan on the moat of Ypres.

II
THE ROADMAKERS

We had just marched from one part of the Front to another and by a round-about way. Each morning the Quartermaster and "the billeting party" went on before, and each evening we slept in a village that was strange to us. Each of the men carried on his back a pack and equipment weighing about eighty or ninety pounds. Through sleet and blizzard and, for the most part, through open, exposed country, we continued our march without a day of rest. By the fifth evening we reached the village where we were to have three or four weeks of rest and training before entering the trenches for the spring offensive. We had unpacked and were sitting at dinner when a telegram came announcing that all previous plans were canceled, and that at dawn we must take to the road again. Something unexpected had happened, good or ill, we knew not which, and we had to enter the line in front of Arras. For three days more we marched. Daily the sound of the guns came nearer, and the men were tired and footsore. They were also deeply disappointed of the long rest to which they had been looking forward after a winter in the trenches at Neuve Chapelle. Yet they marched cheerily enough. "It's the War!" they said one to another and, true to their own philosophy, "packed up their troubles in their old kit bags and smiled." When any man faltered a bit, as if about to fall out by the way, the others cheered him on by singing "Old Soldiers never die" to the tune of the old Sunday school hymn, "Kind words can never die." Sometimes an officer would shoulder a man's rifle to the end of the march, or until he felt better. In eight unbroken days of marching we covered ninety-eight miles and finally arrived at a camp of huts within a day's march of the trenches we are to occupy. Here, where our huts stand like islands in a sea of mud, we are, unless suddenly needed, to take a few days' rest.

On the ninety-eight miles of road over which we tramped, we passed company after company of British roadmakers. In some parts they were widening the road, in other parts repairing it. The roads of Northeastern France are handed over to our care as completely as if they were in England. Our road-makers are everywhere, and as we pass they stand, pick or shovel in hand, to salute the colonel and shout some humorous remark to the laughing riflemen--only to get back as much as they give.

This morning I visited the neighboring village to arrange for a Sunday service. The roads are hopeless for bicycles at this time of the year, so I fell back on Adam's method of getting about. The road to the village was torn and broken, and "thaw precautions" were being observed. Everywhere it was ankle-deep in mud and, in the holes, knee-deep. Innumerable motor-wagons had crushed it beneath their ponderous weight, and my feet had need of my eyes to guide them. In skirting the holes and rough places, I added quite a mile to the journey.

It was annoying to get along so slowly, and I called the road "rotten" and blamed the War for its destructive work. Then I saw that I had been unjust in judgment. The War had constructed more than it had destroyed. The road had been a little muddy country lane, but the soldiers had made it wide as Fleet Street, and it was bearing a mightier traffic than that famous thoroughfare night and day. The little road with its mean perfections and imperfections had gone, and the large road with big faults and big virtues had come. This soldiers' road has faults the farmers' road knew not, but then it has burdens and duties unknown before, and it has had no time to prepare for them. Like our boy-officers who are bearing grown men's burdens of responsibility and bearing them well, the road has had no time to harden. To strengthen itself for its duties, it eats up stones as a giant eats up food. I had no right to look for the smoothness of Oxford Street or the Strand. Such avenues represent the work of centuries, this of days. They have grown with their burdens, but this has had vast burdens thrown upon it suddenly, and while it was immature. Oxford Street and Fleet Street are the roads of peace, and laden with wealth and luxury, law and literature--things that can wait. But on this road of the soldiers' making, nothing is allowed except it be concerned with matters of life and death. It is the road of war, and there is a terrible urgency about it. Over it pass ammunition to the guns, rations to the soldiers in the trenches, ambulances bearing back the wounded to the hospital. Whatever its conditions the work must be done, and there is no room for a halting prudence or the pride of appearance. Rough though it is and muddy, over it is passing, for all who have eyes to see, a new and better civilization and a wider liberty. I had grumbled at the worn-out road when I ought to have praised it. I was as an ingrate who finds fault with his father's hands because they are rough and horny.

It was a group of soldier-roadmakers who brought me to my senses. They were making a new road through the fields, and it branched off from the one I was on. I saw its crude beginning and considered the burdens it would soon have to bear. As I stood watching these English roadmakers my mind wandered down the avenues of time, and I saw the Roman soldiers building their immortal roads through England. They were joining town to town and country to country. They were introducing the people of the North to those of the South, and bringing the East into fellowship with the West. I saw come along their roads the union of all England followed at, some distance, by that of England, Scotland and Wales; and I regretted that there was no foundation on which they could build a road to Ireland. I saw on those soldier-built roads, also, Christianity and Civilization marching, and in the villages and towns by the wayside they found a home whence they have sent out missionaries and teachers to the ends of the earth.

"The captains and the kings depart." The Roman Empire is no more, but the Roman roads remain. They direct our modern life and business with an inevitability the Roman soldiers never exercised. In two thousand years the Empire may have fallen apart and become a thing of the past; but the roads her sons have built in France, these two-and-a-half years, will abide forever and be a perpetual blessing; for, of things made by hands, there is, after the church and the home, nothing more sacred than the road. The roadmaker does more for the brotherhood of man and the federation of the world than the most eloquent orator. The roadmaker has his dreams and visions as well as the poet, and he expresses them in broken stones. He uses stones as artists use colors, and orators words. He touches them--transient as they are--with immortality. A little of his soul sticks to each stone he uses, and though the stone perishes the road remains. His body may perish more quickly than the stones and be laid in some quiet churchyard by the wayside, but his soul will never utterly forsake the road he helped to make. In man's nature, and in all his works, there is a strange blending of the temporal and the eternal, and in nothing is it more marked than in the roads he builds.

The roadmaker is the pioneer among men and without him there would be neither artist nor orator. He goes before civilization as John the Baptist went before Christ, and he is as rough and elemental. Hard as his own stones, without him mankind would have remained savage and suspicious as beasts of prey; and art, science and literature would have had no beginning. His road may begin in war, but it ends in peace.

The pioneers I saw roadmaking were, for the greater part, over military age, and such as I had often seen leaning heavily on the bar of some miserable beer-house. In those days they seemed of the earth, earthy, and the stars that lure to high thoughts and noble endeavors seemed to shine on them in vain. But one never knows what is passing in the heart of another. Of all things human nature is the most mysterious and deceptive. God seems to play at hide-and-seek with men. He hides pearls in oysters lying in the ooze of the sea; and gold under the everlasting snows of the Arctic regions. Diamonds he buries deep down in the dirt beneath the African veldt. He places Christ in a carpenter's shop, Joan of Arc in a peasant's dwelling, Lincoln in a settler's cabin, and Burns in a crude cottage built by his father's own hands. He hides generous impulses and heroic traits in types of men that in our mean imaginations we can only associate with the saw-dust sprinkled bar-room. Only when war or pestilence have kindled their fierce and lurid flames do we find the hidden nobility that God has stored away in strange places--places often as foul and unlikely as those where a miser stores his gold.

When Diogenes went about with a candle in search of an honest man did he think to look in the taverns and slums? I fancy not. Not Diogenes' candle but the "Light of the World" was needed to reveal the treasure God has hidden in men. Christ alone knew where His Father had hidden His wealth and could guide us to it. In this time of peril when every man with any nobility in him is needed to stand in the deadly breach, and with body and soul hold back the brutality and tyranny that would enslave the world we have, like the woman in the parable, lit a candle and searched every corner of our kingdom diligently. In the dust of unswept corners we have found many a coin of value that, but for our exceeding need, would have remained hidden. To me, the wealth and wonder of the war have been found in its sweepings. Time and again we have found those who were lost, and a new happiness has come into life. To the end of my days I shall walk the earth with reverent feet. I did not know men were so great. I have looked at life without seeing the gold through the dust, and have been no better than a Kaffir child playing marbles with diamonds, unaware of their value. I have gone among my fellows with proud step where I ought to have walked humbly, and have rushed in where angels feared to tread.

Life at the Front has made me feel mean among mankind. My comrades have been so great. In days long past, I have trodden on the hem of Christ's garment without knowing it. I have not seen its jewels because I, and others, have so often trodden it in the mire. Yet, through the mire of slum and tavern, the jewels have emerged pearl-white and ruby-red. And I feel that I owe to a large part of mankind an apology for having been before the war so blind, callous and superficial. But for the agony and bloody sweat in which I have seen my fellows, I should never have known them for what they are, and the darkness of death would have covered me before I had realized what made the death of Christ and the sufferings of all the martyrs well worth while. Now there is a new light upon my path and I shall see the features of an angel through the dirt on a slum-child's face. Words of Christ that once lay in the shadow now stand out clearly, for whenever we get below the surface of life we come to *Him*. He is there before us, and awaiting our coming.

I also understand, now, something of the meaning of the words which the Unemployed scrawled upon their banner before the war--"Damn your charity. Give us work." It was a deep and true saying, and taught them by a stern teacher. When the war came we *did* "damn our charity" and gave them "work." Many a man got his first chance of doing "a man's job," and rose to the full height of his manhood. Many hitherto idle and drunken, were touched in their finer parts. They saw their country's need, and though their country had done little to merit their gratitude, they responded to her call before some of the more prudent and sober. Those who were young went out to fight, and every officer can tell stories about their behavior in the hours of danger and suffering which bring tears to the eyes and penitence to the heart. Those above military age went out to make roads over which their younger brothers and sons could march, and get food, ammunition, or an ambulance according to their needs. Among the group of middle-aged roadmakers that I saw there were, I doubt not, some who had been counted wastrels and who had made but a poor show of life. Now they had got work that made them feel that they were men and not mendicants, and they were "making good."

While I watched them a lark rose from a neighboring field and sang over them a song of the coming spring. It was the first lark I had heard this year, and I was glad it mingled its notes with the sounds of the roadmakers' shovels. Nature is not so indifferent to human struggles as it sometimes seems. The man who stands steadfastly by the right and true and bids tyranny and wrong give place will find, at last, that he is in league with the stones of the field and the birds of the air, and that the stars in their courses fight for him. The roadmaker and the lark are born friends. Both are heralds of coming gladness, and while one works, the other sings. True work and pure song are never far apart. They are both born of hope and seek to body forth the immortal. A man works while he has faith. Would he sow if he did not believe the promise, made under the rainbow, that seed-time and harvest shall never fail? Or could he sing with despair choking his heart? Yet he can sing with death choking it. In the very act of dying Wesley sang the hymn, "I'll praise my Maker while I've breath." He sang because of the hope of immortality. He was not turning his face to the blank wall of death and oblivion but to the opening gate of a fuller life. He was soaring sunwards like the lark, and soaring sang,

"And when my voice is lost in death

Praise shall employ my nobler powers;

My days of praise shall ne'er be past."

Joy can sing and Sorrow can sing, but Despair is dumb. It has not even a cry, for a cry is a call for help as every mother knows, and Despair knows no helper. Even the saddest song has hope in it, as the dreariest desert has a well. The loved one is dead but Love lives on and whispers of a trysting place beyond this bourne of time, where loved and lover meet again. The patriot's life may be pouring from a dozen wounds on the muddy field of battle, but his fast-emptying heart is singing with each heavy beat, "Who dies, if my country live?"

Roadmakers have prepared the way for missionaries in every land. Trail-blazers are not always religious men--often they are wild, reckless fellows whom few would allow a place in the Kingdom of God--but is not their work religious in its final upshot? Do they not, however unconsciously, "prepare the way of the Lord, make straight in the desert a highway for our God?" Close on their heels go the missionaries, urged on faster by the pure love of souls than the trader by love of lucre. The greatest among the roadmakers was a missionary himself--David Livingstone. And for such an one the name Living-stone is perfect. It has the touch of destiny. Through swamp and forest he went where white feet had never trod, and blazed a trail for the messengers of Christ, until, worn out with fever and hardship, he fell asleep at his prayers, to wake no more to toil and suffering.

But while the roadmaker bestows benefits on us he also lays obligations, for there can be no enlargement of privilege without a corresponding increase of responsibility. The roads the men are making here in France will be good for trade. They will open up the country as did the military roads of Caesar and Napoleon; and along them soldiers are marching who, at tremendous cost to themselves, are buying for posterity great benefits, and laying upon posterity great obligations. Posterity must hold and enlarge the liberties won for them, and prove worthy of their citizenship by resisting tyranny "even unto blood." We are here because our fathers were heroes and lovers of liberty. Had they been cowards and slaves there would have been no war for us. As we follow our fathers our sons must be ready to follow us. The present springs out of the past, and the future will spring out of the present. Inheritance implies defense on the part of the inheritors.

The very names they give to their roads show that our soldiers have grasped this fact. The cold canvas hut in which I am writing is officially described as No. 1 Hut, *Oxford* Street. A little farther off, and running parallel with it, is *Cambridge* Road. There is also an *Eton* Road, *Harrow* Road, and *Marlborough* Road. Students of the universities and schools after which these roads are named are out here to defend what these institutions have stood for through the hoary centuries. They are out to preserve the true conception of Liberty and Fair-play, and to build roads along which all peoples who desire it can travel unmolested by attacks from either tyrants or anarchists.

Right from the beginning of the war, the idea of a Road has taken hold of the imagination of our soldiers. The first divisions came out singing, "It's a long, long way to Tipperary, but my heart's right there." Nowadays the popular song is "There's a long, long trail awinding into the Land of my dreams."

They are making a Road of Liberty along which all nations may pass to universal peace and brotherhood, and where the weak will be as safe from oppression as the strong. "It's a long, long way to go," but they have seen their goal on the horizon, and will either reach it or die on the way to it. They have made up their minds that never again shall the shadow of the Kaiser's mailed fist, or that any other tyrant fall across their path. These men never sing of war. They hate war. It is a brutal necessity forced on them by the ambition of a tyrant. Their songs are all of peace and none of war. Of the future and not the present they sing:

"Tiddley-iddley-ighty,

Hurry me home to Blighty;

Blighty is the place for me."

Whether they sing with levity or seriousness (and levity of manner often veils their seriousness of feeling), it is of a future of peace and goodwill they sing. To them the war is a hard road leading to a better life for mankind. It is to them what the desert was to the Israelites, when they left the bondage of Egypt for the liberty of the Land of Promise. Therefore they must tread it without faltering even as Christ trod the way of the Cross. "There's a long, long trail awinding into the Land of their dreams" and they will not lose faith in their dreams however wearisome the way. Elderly navvies and laborers have come to smooth the roads for them, and nurses are tending those who have fallen broken by the way; while across the sundering sea are mothers and wives whose prayers make flowers spring up at their feet and blossoms break out on every tree that fringes the side of the road.

III
THE GLAMOUR OF THE FRONT

There is an undoubted glamour about the Front, which when at home, in England, cannot be explained. In the army or out of it, the wine of life is white and still, but at the Front it runs red and sparkling. One day I got a lift in a motor-wagon and sat on a box by the side of one of the servants of the officer's mess at the Aerodrome near by. He was going into Doullens, a market town, to buy food and some little luxuries. Captain Ball, V.C., the prince of English flyers, was, up to the time of his death in the air, a member of the mess, and the servant was telling me how comfortable all the officers make their quarters. In a phrase he defined the glamour of the Front.

"One day," he said, "when we were helping him to make his room comfortable, Captain Ball burst out into a merry laugh and chuckled, 'We haven't long to live, but we live well while we do live.'"

There you have it. Life is concentrated. Death is near--just round the corner--so the men make the most of their time and "live well." It has the same quality as "leave" at home. Leave is short and uncertain, so we "live well." Our friends know it may be the last sight of us, and we know it may be our last sight of them. They are kind and generous to us, as we are to them; and so, the ten days of "leave" are just glorious. Ruskin says that the full splendor of the sunset lasts but a second, and that Turner went out early in the evening and watched with rapt attention for that one second of supreme splendor and delight. He lived for sunsets and while others were balancing their accounts, or taking tea, he went out to see the daily miracle. The one second in which he saw God pass by in the glory of the sunset was to him worth all the twenty-four hours. For one second in each day he caught the glamour of earth and heaven, and went back to his untidy studios blind to all but the splendor he had seen.

That second each day was life, indeed, and the glamour of the Front is like unto it. It is the place where life sets, and the darkness of death draws on. The commonest soldier feels it and with true instinct, not less true because unconscious, he describes death at the Front as "going West." It is the presence of death that gives the Front its glamour, and life its concentrated joy and fascination. Captain Ball saw it with the intuition of genius when he said: "We haven't long to live, but we live well while we *do* live."

The immediate presence of death at the Front gives tone to every expression of life, and makes it the kindest place in the world. No one feels he can do too much for you, and there is nothing you would not do for another. Whether you are an officer or a private, you can get a lift on any road, in any vehicle, that has an inch of room in it. How often have I seen a dozen tired Tommies clambering up the back of an empty motor-lorry which has stopped, or slowed down, to let them get in. It is one of the merriest sights of the war and redounds to the credit of human nature. Cigarettes are passed round by those who have, to those who have not, with a generosity that reminds one of nothing so much as that of the early Christians who "had all things common; and sold their possessions and goods, and parted them to all men, as every man had need." You need never go hungry while others have food. Officers are welcome at every mess they go near, and privates will get food in the servants' kitchen or may go shares with the men in any billet. It may be a man's own fault that he took no food on the march, and his comrades may tell him so in plain strong language, but they will compel him to share what they have just the same.

One wet night on the Somme I got lost in "Happy Valley" and could not find my regiment. Seeing a light in a tent, I made for it. It was a pioneers' tent, but they invited me to come in out of the storm and stay the night. They were at supper and had only a small supply of bully-beef, biscuits and strong tea; but they insisted on me sharing what they had. I was dripping with rain, and they gave me one of their blankets. One of them gave me a box to sleep on, while he shared his chum's. Some lost privates came in later wet to the skin, and the pioneers gave them all the eatables left over from supper, and shared out their blankets and clothes. It was pure Christianity--whatever creeds they may think they believe. And it is the glamour of the Front. England feels cold and dull after it. Kindness and comradeship pervade the air in France. You feel that everyone is a friend and brother. It will be pretty hard for chaplains to go back to their churches. They have been spoiled by too much kindness. How can they go back to the cold atmosphere of criticism and narrow judgments which prevail in so many churches--that is, unless the war has brought changes there also? And after preaching to dying men who listen as it their destiny depended upon their hearing, how can they go back to pulpits where large numbers in the congregations regard their messages as of less importance than dinner, and as merely supplying material for an exercise in more or less kindly criticism during the discussion of that meal?

The glamour of the services at the Front! How the scenes are photographed on my heart! As a congregation sits in a church at home how stolid its features often are--how dull its eyes! One glance around and the preacher's heart sinks within him and his inspiration flies away. Nothing is expected of him, and nothing particularly desired. People have come by force of habit, and not of need. But how the eyes of the soldiers in France glow and burn; how their features speak, and make the preacher speak in reply! Who could help being eloquent there! Such faces would make the dumb speak. One can see the effect of his words as plainly in their expressions as he can see the effect of wind on a cornfield. Every emotion from humor to concern leaps from the heart to the face as the subject touches them at, first this point of their life, then at that. The men's eyes are unforgettable. Months afterwards they come vividly to mind, and one is back again answering the questions they silently ask, and seeing the look of content or gratitude that takes the place of the perplexed or troubled expression. Eyes are said to be the windows of the soul, and as I have spoken I have seen men's souls looking out. At home the windows are darkened and there seemed to be no souls behind the panes. The dwellers within the houses are busy with other matters, and will not come to the windows. The preacher feels like an organ-grinder in the street--those who hear do not heed nor come to the windows of the soul. In France there is a soul looking out at every window; and the preacher sings--for his words grow rhythmic--to his listeners of the love of God and of the love of women and children which make sweet this vale of tears and light man on his lone way beyond the grave.

One Sunday in hospital, when we heard the singing of a hymn in the ward below, a young officer, in the next bed, turned to me and said: "Why doesn't the chaplain hold a service for us? Why does he only hold them for the Tommies? We need them and want them, just as much as the Tommies. We are officers but we are also men." I passed the word to the chaplain, and he was a joyful man when in the evening he gave us a service and the officers of the next ward asked the orderlies to carry them in.

There is the same naturalness and spirit of fellowship between members of various churches. Many lasting friendships have been formed between chaplains of differing communions. There has been no change of creed but something greater, a change of spirit. They have been touched by the common spirit, and have lived and worked in free and happy fellowship. On my last Sunday in a hospital in France, the chaplain, a canon of the Church of England, invited me to read the lesson at the morning parade service, and to administer the wine at Holy Communion. This I did; and a colonel who was present stayed behind to express to us both the pleasure which had been given to him by the sight of Anglican and Methodist churchmen serving together at the Lord's Table.

To a chaplain not a little of the glamour of the Front is found in this warm fellowship between men of differing creeds and varying religious communions. We have not knocked down our garden walls but we have taken off the cut glass that had been cemented on them by our fathers; and now we can lean over and talk to our neighbors. We have already found that our neighbors are human beings, and quite normal. The chief difference between us seems to be that while one has an obsession for roses the other has an obsession for dahlias. On pansies, sweet peas and chrysanthemums we seem equally keen and exchange plants. A Roman Catholic officer who had been appointed to the Ulster Division told me that though he was received coldly at first, he had not been with the Division more than a few weeks when every officer in his regiment, and every soldier in his company, accepted him as cordially as if he were a Protestant. He was from Dublin and they from Belfast, but they did not allow it to make any difference, and feelings of the warmest loyalty and friendship sprang up. His Tommies would fight to the death by his side, as readily as around any Ulsterman; and he was just as popular in the officers' mess. When, he said, it passed the Irish Guards or any other Roman Catholic regiment, his regiment would sing some provoking song about "hanging the Pope with a good strong rope," and the Dublin regiment would reply with some song equally obnoxious and defiant; but whereas, in peace time, the songs would have caused a free fight to the accompaniment of bloodshed, now it caused nothing worse than laughter. The songs were just a bit of teasing such as every regiment likes to regale another with-- perhaps, too, a common memory of the dear country they have left behind. The men of Belfast and the men of Dublin have learned to respect and value one another. They know that in a scrap with the enemy they can count on one another to the last drop of blood, for, whether from North or South, the Irish are "bonnie fighters." Of such are the miracles at the Front.

Most of all, perhaps, the glamour of the Front is found in the nobility to which common men rise. An artillery officer told me that he had in his battery a soldier who seemed utterly worthless. He was dirty in all his ways, and unreliable in character. In despair they made him sanitary orderly, that is, the scavenger whose duty it was to remove all refuse. One night the officer wanted a man to go on a perilous errand and there were few men available. Instantly this lad volunteered. The officer looked at him in amazement, and with a reverence born on the instant. "No," he thought, "I will not let him go and get killed. I'll go myself." He told the lad so, and disappointment was plainly written on his features.

"But, you'll let me come with you, sir?" he replied.

"Why should two risk their lives," asked the officer, "when one can do the job?"

"But you might get wounded, sir," was the quick response; and they went together.

An Irish officer told me of one man who seemed bad from top to toe. All the others had some redeeming feature but this man appeared not to possess any. He used the filthiest language and was dirty in his habits and dress. He was drunken and stole the officers' whisky out of the mess. He was unchaste and had been in the hospital with venereal disease; and neither as man nor soldier was there anything good to say of him. The regiment was sent to France, and in due time took its place in the trenches; and then appeared in this man something that had never risen to the surface before. Wherever there were wounded and dying men he proved himself to be the noblest man in the regiment. When a man fell in No Man's Land, he was over the parapet in the twinkling of an eye to bring him in. No barrage could keep him away from the wounded. It was a sort of passion with him that nothing could restrain. To save others he risked his life scores of times. In rest-billets he would revert to some of his evil ways, but in the trenches he was the Greatheart of the regiment and, though he did not receive it, he earned the Victoria Cross over and over again. There is a glamour at the Front that holds the heart with an irresistible grip. In the light of War's deathly fires the hearts of men are revealed and the black sheep often get their chance. Life is intense and deep and men are drawn together by a common peril. They find the things that unite and forget the things that separate.

"We haven't long to live," said Captain Ball joyfully, "but we live well while we *do* live," and in those words he expressed the glamour of the Front. Ball found, as thousands of his comrades-in-arms had found, that

"One crowded hour of glorious life

Is worth an age without a name."

IV
A WHITE HANDKERCHIEF

In his *History of the Somme Campaign* John Buchan quotes, from an official report, an incident which, though I have tried, I cannot get my imagination to believe. Probably the incident is a true one but, unfortunately for me, my mind will not let it in. I cannot visualize it and the report is turned from the door as an impostor. The report states that in a certain attack our aeroplanes fired on the Germans in their trenches and that the enemy waved white handkerchiefs in token of surrender. Without the slightest difficulty I can imagine all except the white handkerchiefs. Where did they get them to wave? Men in the firing trenches don't carry anything so conspicuous as white handkerchiefs. To draw one out in a thoughtless moment might bring a sniper's bullet, and there are risks enough without inviting more. I doubt if in any English regiment two white handkerchiefs could be found: and I have little expectation that more could be found among the enemy. Furthermore, it is questionable, at this stage of the war, if a white handkerchief would be regarded as a sign, of surrender. It might be taken as a taunt.

There is nothing more remarkable in the war than the psychological change that has been wrought in white. A white feather used to be the badge of cowardice and a white flag the token of surrender. It is not so now. White has taken on a peculiar sacredness. If a new medal were to be struck of the same high value as the Victoria Cross it would probably be given a white ribbon, as the other has a red or (for the navy) blue. This change in the moral significance of white was brought home to me by an incident in a billet. I had gone to a barn to give the men some shirts and socks that had been sent to me. I stood on the steps, and like an auctioneer, offered my goods for acceptance. "Who wants a shirt? Who a scarf? Who wants this pair of mittens? Who a pair of socks?" Hands shot up at each question, and the fun grew fast and furious. Then I drew out and held up a white handkerchief. "A-ah! A-ah!" they cried wistfully in chorus. For a moment they stood gazing at it and forgot to raise their hands towards it; then, with a single movement, every hand shot up. Unwittingly I had stirred them to the depths; and I felt sorry for them.

The Magic Carpet of Baghdad is not a fiction after all. In the twinkling of an eye my white handkerchief had carried every boy and man to his home, and placed him by the fireside. I saw it in their eyes and heard it in the sadness and wistfulness of their voices as they ejaculated "A-ah!" They had not seen a white handkerchief for months. The last they saw was at home. A vision of home flashed before their minds and they were back in the dear old days of peace when they used white handkerchiefs and khaki ones were unknown to them. If in battle they were to see Germans waving white handkerchiefs, I think it would make them savage and unwilling to give quarter. They would think the enemy was taunting them with all they had lost. And they would be maddened by the thought that here were the very men who, by their war-lust, had caused them to lose it. For a German to wave a white handkerchief before a British soldier would be as dangerous as flaunting a red flag before a bull. It would bring death rather than pity. Anything of pure white is rare at the front, and it has gradually taken on a meaning it never held before. About the only white thing we have is the paper we write home on, and that use of the color helps to sanctify it in the shrine of the heart.

In the army it is a term of supreme praise to call a man *white*. When you say a comrade is a "*white man*" there is no more to be said. It is worth more than the Victoria Cross with its red ribbon, for it includes gallantry, and adds to it goodness. A man must be brave to be called white and he must be generous, noble and good. To reach whiteness is a great achievement. To be dubbed white is, in the army, like being dubbed knight at King Arthur's Court or canonized saint in the Church. He stands out among a soldier's comrades distinct as a white handkerchief among khaki ones.

I don't know where the term came from, but, wherever it may have tarried on the way, I think its footprints could be traced back to the Book of Revelation for its starting place. In the first chapter we have a picture of Christ as the first "White Man"--"His Head and His Hairs were white like wool, as white as snow." In the second chapter His faithful followers are given "a white stone, and in the stone a new name written." Is not the new name "White man"? In the third chapter we read of "a few names even in Sardis which have *not defiled their garments*; and they shall *walk with Me in white*; for they are worthy." There, too, the Laodiceans are counseled to buy "white raiment." In the fourth chapter we see the four and twenty elders, sitting around the throne under the rainbow arch, "clothed in white raiment." In the sixth chapter we have the crowned King going "forth conquering, and to conquer" and He is sitting on "a white horse," that is, He uses "white" instruments to carry out His conquests. Death, in the same chapter, rides on a "pale" horse, but not a "white" one. Under the altar were the souls of the martyrs, "And white robes were given unto every one of them." And surely the climax is reached when we read in the seventh chapter that "a great multitude, which no man could number, of all nations, and kindreds, and people and tongues, stood before the throne, and before the Lamb, clothed with white robes." So striking was the scene that one of the elders asked, "What are these which are arrayed in white robes? and whence came they?" And the answer is given, "These are they which came out of great tribulation, and have washed their robes, and made them white in the blood of the Lamb. Therefore are they before the throne of God." In the army white has come back to its ancient significance. The brave and noble martyrs of the early Church were given "white robes" and in the army to-day the brave and pure wear "white robes" in the eyes of their comrades. When Clifford Reed was killed by a shell at his Regimental Aid Post his colonel wrote of him that he was the "whitest man" he had ever known. He had done more than wear "the white flower of a *blameless* life." His virtues were positive, not merely negative. He wore a "white *robe*"; not a mere speck of white such as a white flower in a buttonhole would appear. White is a positive color, not a negative. Reed was more than "blameless," he was "white and all white." To our soldiers a white handkerchief speaks of home, and a "white man" speaks of honor and heroism and heaven.

V
THE SONGS OUR SOLDIERS SING

The necessity for poetry and song is fully and officially recognized by the military authorities at the Front. Every Division has its own concert party. These men are chosen out of the ranks because they can sing, and their one task is to furnish nightly concerts for the men. They are provided with a good hall, or tent, or open-air position; and they are given enough money to buy stage scenery and appropriate dress. Everybody attends the concerts from the general to the private; and while the entertainments last, the war is forgotten. A charge is made at the door but the balance sheet is published for all ranks to see; and the profits are distributed among the Divisional charities.

Among the many Divisional Concert Parties may be named "The Bow Bells," "The Duds," "The Follies," "The Whizz-bangs," "The Fancies" and, "The Giddigoats." But, after all, the singing in the concert rooms is but a small fraction of the singing one hears in the Army. On every march, in every billet and mess, there is the sound of singing. Nor must the singing at our religious services and in the Y.M.C.A. huts be forgotten. Song seems to be the great renewer of hope and courage. It is the joy bringer. Moreover, it is an expression of emotions that can find no other voice.

There is no real difference between the songs sung by the officers, and those sung by the men. All attend the concerts and all sing on the march. The same songs do for both commanders and commanded, and I have heard the same songs in the men's billets as in the officers' mess-rooms. How real these songs are to the soldiers is indicated by one striking omission. There are no patriotic songs at the Front. Except the National Anthem rendered on formal occasions, I have never, in eighteen months, heard a single patriotic song. The reason is not far to seek. The soldiers' patriotism calls for no expression in song. They are expressing it night and day in the endurance of hardship and wounds--in the risking of their lives. Their hearts are satisfied with their deeds, and songs of such a character become superfluous. In peace-time they sing their love of the homeland, but in war-time they suffer for her and are content. They would never think of singing a patriotic song as they march into battle. It would be painting the lily and gilding refined gold. Are not their deathless deeds, songs for which they make a foil by singing some inconsequential and evanescent song such as, "There's something in the sea-side air."

On analysis I should say that there are five subjects on which our soldiers sing. First, there are Nonsense Songs or, if you prefer it, songs of soldier-philosophy. They know that no theory will explain the war; it is too big a thing for any sheet of philosophy to cover. It has burst in on our little hum-drum life like a colliding planet. The thing to do is not to evolve a theory as to how the planet got astray but to clear up the mess it has made. Our soldiers show this sense of the vastness of war-happenings, by singing of things having no real importance at all, and keeping steadily at their duties. The path of duty is, they find, the only path of sanity. The would-be war philosopher they put on one side. The war is too big for him. Let him leave his explanation of the war and lend a hand to bring it to an end. So they sing, with laughing irony,

"We're here because we're here, because
We're here, because we're here."

Or,

"While you've got a lucifer to light your fag,
Smile, boys, that's the style.
What's the use of worrying?
It never was worth while,
So pack up your troubles in your old kit-bag
And smile, smile, smile."

Another favorite is,

"Oh, there was a little hen and she had a wooden leg,
The best little hen that ever laid an egg,
And she laid more eggs than any hen on the farm,
And another little drink wouldn't do us any harm."

I have seen them dancing round some old piano singing,

"Oh, that fascinating Bow Bells' glide,

It's a captivating Bow Bells' slide.

There's a rumor that the puma does it now,

Monkeys have taken to it,

Leopards and lions do it.

All the elephants wear dancing shoes,

They keep hopping with the kangaroos;

Hear them chatter, it's a matter for some talk;

Now the Jungle's got the Bow Bells' walk."

The second class of song is the Love Song, of a more or less serious character. The Tommies came out of England singing "Tipperary," but they dropped it in France, and the only one on whose lips I have heard it was a little French boy sitting on the tail of a cart. The chorus alone gave it popularity for it was the expression, ready to hand, of a long farewell; and with its "long long way to go" showed that, like Kitchener, the soldiers were not deceived by hopes of an early peace.

Now another song with verses more expressive of their sentiments has taken its place. The chorus runs:

"There's a long, long trail a-winding

Into the land of my dreams,

Where the nightingales are singing

And a white moon beams;

There's a long, long night of waiting

Until my dreams all come true;

Till the day when I'll be going down

That long, long trail with you."

Then the mood changes, and we hear the lads piping out,

"Taffy's got his Jennie in Glamorgan,

Sandy's got his Maggie in Dundee,

While Michael O'Leary thinks of his dearie

Far across the Irish Sea.
Billy's got his Lily up in London,
So the boys march on with smiles;
For every Tommy's got a girl somewhere
In the dear old British Isles."

Again the mood veers round, and we hear,

"Every little while I feel so lonely,
Every little while I feel so blue,
I'm always dreaming, I'm always scheming,
Because I want you, and only you.
Every little while my heart is aching,
Every little while I miss your smile,
And all the time I seem to miss you;
I want to, want to kiss you,
Every, every, every little while."

Here is part of a song I have heard sung, many and many a time, by young
officers and men whose voices are now silent in death:

"If you were the only girl in the world,
And I were the only boy,
Nothing else would matter in the world to-day,
We could go on loving in the same old way;
A Garden of Eden just made for two,
With nothing to mar our joy;
I would say such wonderful things to you,
There would be such wonderful things to do,
If you were the only girl in the world,
And I were the only boy."

Sometimes the imagination will wander into the days that are to be--for some--and they sing,

"We don't want a lot of flags flying,

We don't want your big brass bands;

We don't want a lot of speechifying,

And we don't want a lot of waving hands;

We don't want a lot of interfering,

When we've safely crossed the foam;

But we *do* want to find the girls we left behind,

When we all come marching home."

Will the girls remember! The words are not without tragedy. How deeply some of the men love may perhaps never be realized by those at home. The longing of their hearts is, at times, almost unbearable. A captain, past middle life, took my arm one day and led me aside. He was, he said, a little anxious about himself, for he was getting into the habit of taking more drink than he was wont to take. He had been taking it when he felt lonely and depressed to ease the longing of his heart.

"I never touch it at home," he said, "the society of my dear little wife is all the stimulant I need. I would give the world to be with her now--just to sit in my chair and watch her at her sewing or knitting. The separation is too much for me and, you know, it has lasted nearly three years now."

I have caught this yearning in more than one of the songs our soldiers sing, but especially in the following, which is called "Absent":

"Sometimes, between long shadows on the grass,

The little truant waves of sunlight pass;

My eyes grow dim with tenderness, the while

Thinking I see thee, thinking I see thee smile.

"And sometimes in the twilight gloom, apart,

The tall trees whisper, whisper heart to heart;

From my fond lips the eager answers fall,

Thinking I hear thee, thinking I hear thee call."

The men's thoughts pass easily from the sweetheart to the mother who bore them, and we have a third class, the Home Song. I have been awakened in the night by men, going up to the line, singing "Keep the Home Fires Burning." It is very thrilling to hear in the dead of night, when every singer is within range of the enemy's guns.

Another great favorite is,

"They built a little garden for the rose,

And they called it Dixie-land;

They built a summer breeze to keep the snows

Far away from Dixie-land;

They built the finest place I've known,

When they built my home sweet home;

Nothing was forgotten in the land of cotton,

From the clover to the honey-comb,

And then they took an angel from the skies

And they gave her heart to me.

She had a bit of heaven in her eyes

Just as blue as blue can be;

They put some fine spring chickens in the land,

And taught my Mammy how to use a frying pan.

They made it twice as nice as paradise,

And they called it Dixie-land."

Being Londoners, the following song called "Leave" never fails in its appeal to our Division:

"I'm so delighted, I'm so excited,

With my folks I'm going to be united.

The train's departing, 'twill soon be starting;

I'll see my mother, my dad and my baby brother.

My! How I'll meet them, My! how I'll greet them.

What a happy happy day.

Just see that bustle, I'd better hustle,

Good-bye--so long--can't stay--

Chorus

"I'm on my way back to dear old Shepherd's Bush,

That's the spot where I was born,

Can't you hear the porter calling,

Queen's Road, Piccadilly, Marble Arch and Bond Street?

Oh, I'll not hesitate, I'll reach the gate;

Through the crowd I mean to push,

Find me a seat anywhere--please anywhere,

Tram, train, tube, 'bus I don't care--

For mother and daddy are waiting there--

In dear old Shepherd's Bush."

On the eve of one big battle, a soldier handed me a letter in which he gave me the addresses of his father and his sweetheart, so that I could write to them if he fell.

"In the last battle," he said, "one of my brothers was killed and another wounded. If I fall I shall die without regrets and with a heart content; but it will go hard with those at home; and I want you to break the news gently. These are terrible times for those at home." "These are terrible times *for those at home.*" That is their constant refrain, and it finds an echo in a song often sung by them.

"It's a long long way to my home in Kentucky,

Where the blue-bells grow 'round the old cabin door;

It's a long, long way and I'll be mighty lucky

When I see my dear old mammy once more.

So weep no more, my lady,

Just brush those tears away;

It's a long long way to my home in Kentucky,

But I'm bound to get there some day."

But the chief favorite of all Home Songs is, I think, the following:

"There's an old-fashioned house in an old-fashioned street;

In a quaint little old-fashioned town;

There's a street where the cobble stones harass the feet,

As it straggles up hill and then down;

And, though to and fro through the world I must go,

My heart while it beats in my breast,

Where e'er I may roam, to that old-fashioned home

Will fly like a bird to its nest.

"In that old-fashioned house in that old-fashioned street,

Dwell a dear little old-fashioned pair;

I can see their two faces so tender and sweet,

And I love every wrinkle that's there.

I love ev'ry mouse in that old-fashioned house

In the street that runs up hill and down;

Each stone and each stick, ev'ry cobble and brick,

In that quaint little old-fashioned town."

The charm of the Army is its comradeship. Our soldiers have left their homes and friends but they have found new friends, and some of the friendships have become very precious. Men slept side by side in barn and trench, cooked their rations at the same little wood fire, and stood together in the hour of danger and imminent death. Many of them owe their lives to their comrades. There are few songs that express this wonderful comradeship, but there is one that is known and sung through the army. It represents the Songs of Comradeship:

"When you come to the end of a perfect day,

And you sit alone with your thought,

While the chimes ring out with a carol gay,

For the joy that the day has brought;

Do you think what the end of a perfect day

Can mean to a tired heart,

When the sun goes down with a flaming ray,

And the dear friends have to part?

"Well, this is the end of a perfect day,

Near the end of a journey too;

But it leaves a thought that is big and strong,

With a wish that is kind and true.

For mem'ry has painted this perfect day

With colors that never fade;

And we find at the end of a perfect day

The soul of a friend we've made."

The fifth class of song is that of the inner life. It is the Religious Hymn. The soldiers are extremely fond of hymns in their services. You cannot give them too many. "Rock of Ages," "Jesus lover of my soul," "Fight the good fight," "There is a green hill," "At even ere the sun was set," "O God our help in ages past," and "Eternal Father strong to save" cannot be chosen too often. But there are two hymns which have stood out above all others; they are "Abide with me," and "When I survey the wondrous Cross."

There is nothing written by the hand of man which can compete with these two in the blessing and strength which they have brought to our soldiers, especially during an offensive when death has cast his shadow over the hearts of all. During the bitterest weeks in the Somme fighting there was scarcely a service in which we did not sing "When I survey the wondrous Cross." With its assurance of redemption it gave comfort in the face of death. It also gave, for an example, the Supreme Sacrifice.

Some of the songs I have quoted look bare and ungainly as trees in winter, but when the musician has clothed them with music and the singer added to them a touch of his own personality they are fair as trees in summer. Still the fact remains that none of these songs will live on their own merits. They are not born to immortality. Like the daisies they have their day and pass away to make room for others. It is best so. There is not room in the world for everything to be immortal, and the transient has a work of its own to do. The charm and rare beauty of the English countryside are due to the transience of its flowers and foliage and little of the evergreen is enough. We tire of the eternal. The transient songs I have quoted here have been meat and drink to our soldiers in the most terrible war ever waged. They may be poor stuff in comparison with our classic songs but a good appetite can get nourishment out of plain food and grow strong on it. For the purpose in hand these songs have been better than the classics; otherwise they would not have been chosen. There is a time and place for all things. The robin may not be compared with the nightingale but it is not the less welcome, for it sings when the nightingale is silent. Our soldiers' songs will die, some are already dead, but they have done their work and justified their existence. They have given pleasure and strength to men as they went out to do immortal deeds. No wounded soldier, or parched traveler, thinks lightly of a cup of water because it perished in the using; and so it is with the songs our soldiers sing.

VI
EASTER SUNDAY

Night and day for a week, the fearful bombardment continued. Our guns were everywhere, and belching forth without intermission. Dumps of shells were almost as common as sheaves in a corn-field, and processions of ammunition-wagons piled the shells up faster than the gorging guns could take them. The noise was something beyond imagination. It was as though all the devils in hell had come out to demoniacally celebrate the end of the world. We were living--two transport officers and I--in an empty farm-house that, some time before we came in, had been a target for direct hits. One shell had gone through the roof, and another through the gable wall. The windows had been shattered, and the garden and fields were pitted with shell-holes. Our first care had been to look at the cellar, but we had decided, if things became too hot, to make for the open fields. We all slept in the same room, and were at times wakened up by "an arrival" and passed an opinion as to its distance. If, for a time, none came nearer, we turned over and went to sleep again, for a man must sleep even though it be on the edge of a volcano.

One morning the servants found a shell nose-cap beneath the window--just that, and nothing more. The week was wearing on. Another morning some of the 7th Middlesex Regiment were in the baths in the village over the way, and a company of the London Scottish was passing by. Two shells fell in the road. The bathers scampered out of the bath and ran naked, here and there, for shelter; the Scottish "scattered"; but some forty-five soldiers, mostly kilted, lay in the road dead or wounded. In the dead of night a party of machine gunners, just returned from the firing-trench, stood outside their billet in our village square debating if they should make a cup of tea before turning in to sleep. A shell decided the matter, and, next morning, I laid two of them to rest in the little cemetery, and the others stood by as mourners.

The week of terror reached its crisis on the Sunday--an Easter Sunday never to be forgotten. The infantry of the Brigade had been away to a camp, beyond range, for a week's rest. They had now returned ready for the battle. Three of the regiments had taken up their positions in the reserve trenches, but my own regiment was quartered in the fatal village. The day dawned bright and fair, but its smiles were the smiles of a deceiver. The Germans had decided on the destruction of the village, a sort of devil's "hail-and-farewell" before being driven back at the points of bayonets. We were awakened by the firing of machine-guns over our heads, and rushed to the door to see a fight in the air. High up in the blue, two aeroplanes circled about for positions of vantage, and then rushed at one another like hawks in mortal combat. A silence followed. Then one rose and made off towards the battle-line but fell to a shot of our gunners before it could reach safety. The other, with its petrol-tank on fire, was planing down to earth. Down and down an invisible spiral staircase it seemed to rush, while the golden fire burnt at its vitals, and a trailing cloud of smoke marked its path of doom. Breathlessly we watched its descent. It was under perfect control, but its path to the ground was too long and spiral, and the faster it rushed through the air the greater the draught became and the more madly the flames leapt up. Every second was precious and the certainty of its doom made us sick. We saw the body of the observer fall out, and still the flaming machine pursued its course. Then the wings fell away and twirled to the ground like feathers, while the engine and the pilot dropped like a stone. When the bodies were picked up, it was found that the observer had been shot through the head, and that the pilot, with his dead comrade behind him, had worked the wheel until the furious encroaching flame had swept over him, and robbed him of mortal life.

Shells were now dropping in the village every few minutes. Our farm-house was on the right wing, and we stood watching the bombardment. With each burst there rose a cloud of black smoke and red brick-dust, and we knew that another cottage has been destroyed. Then the shells began to creep round to the right as if the enemy was feeling for the bridge over which the ammunition wagons were passing. On one side of the little bridge was a white bell-tent, and we watched the shells dropping within a few feet of it without destroying it. Between the tent and our street lay a stagnant pool, and we saw about a dozen shells fall in its water. The range was lengthening and it seemed as if some invisible octopus were stretching out its feelers towards us. A shell smashed against the farm-house at the bottom of our street. The deadly thing was coming nearer. Some of our sergeants were in a farm-house a few doors away, and, hearing a shell fall in the field between them and the pool, they came to the decision that the moment had come "to scatter," but they were too late. It would have been better had they stayed indoors. As they rushed out a shell burst over the yard three of them fell to the ground dead, and three more were blown back into the house by the force of the explosion. The coping stone of the outhouse where the shell burst was blown away and three ragged seams were scored on the green doorway of the yard outside which the three lads lay dead. One of them had, ten days before, shown me to my billet thirty yards farther up. He acted as interpreter to the regiment and as he had not to go into the line, we thought that he was one of those who would see the end of the war. Yet there he lay.

But the worst calamity of the day was yet to befall. Some fifteen or sixteen ammunition wagons, unable to get through the village, had halted in the Square--"Wipers Square" it had been named. Each wagon was loaded with nine-point-two shells. An enemy-shot fell on a wagon and set it on fire; then the village became like unto Sodom and Gomorrah on their day of doom. One or two drivers bravely stuck to their wagons, and got them out but the rest of the wagons were lost. The scene that followed was indescribable. Doré could never have pictured such horrors. The wagons all caught fire and their loads of shells began to explode. We stood out in the fields and watched the conflagration, while all the time the Germans continued to shell the village. The large village-hall and the houses on each side of the square were utterly destroyed. Great explosions sent fragments of wagons and houses sky-high, and showers of missiles fell even where we stood. The fore part of one wagon was blown on to the roof of a house. Houses caught fire and blazed all afternoon. Some machine-gunners joined us and told how, when choking smoke began to penetrate into their cellar they had to rush through the square and its bursting shells to preserve their lives. A German shell burst in a billet where a platoon of our men were sheltering in the cellar, and those who were not killed by the shell were crushed to death by the fall of the house. Another shell hit the roof of the house in the cellar of which was our Advanced Dressing Station for the morrow's battle. Two orderlies who happened to be in the street were killed, and the colonel was knocked down. In the cellars of almost every house were soldiers or civilians, and all day the ammunition wagons continued burning; shell after shell getting red hot and exploding.

All day the German bombardment continued and, amid a terrific din, our own gunners returned a score or more for every one received. By the bridge another long line of loaded ammunition wagons stood for two hours, and though shells were bursting close by, not one hit the wagons. The drivers stood by them and, as soon as the road was cleared, got them away to the guns. Yet, while the Square was burning and the German shells falling, hundreds of men from the London regiments entered the village from the right, and crossed the bridge to stack their packs so as to be ready for the coming battle. They walked in single file and with wide gaps between, but not a man ran or quickened his pace. My blood tingled with pride at their courage and anger at their carelessness. What *would* make a British soldier run? An officer was walking near the pool. A shell fell near enough for fragments to kill him, but he merely looked round, stopped to light a cigarette and walked leisurely on as if nothing had happened. Three men stood with their backs against a small building near the bridge as if sheltering from the rain. Several shells fell uncomfortably near, so, concluding that the rain had changed its direction, they moved round the corner. And it was not till more shells had fallen near them that they condescended to move away altogether.

Yet this was not bravado for, so far as they knew, no one was watching them. It was due to a certain dignity peculiar to our fighting man. He is too proud to acknowledge defeat. He is a man, and whether any one is watching or not, he is not going to run away from a shell. Hundreds of lives must have been lost through this stubborn pride but, on the other hand, thousands of lives must have been saved by it, for it makes the Army absolutely proof against panic, than which, nothing is so fatal in war. In eighteen months on the Front I have never seen or heard of a single case of panic either with many or few. Our soldiers are always masters of themselves. They have the coolness to judge what is the wisest thing to do in the circumstances, and they have the nerve to carry it out. They run unnecessary risks through pride but never through panic. All that day on the bridge, a military policeman stood at his post of duty. Like Vesuvius of old the exploding shells in the Square sent up their deadly eruption, and like the Roman sentry at Pompeii, he stood at his post. As he stood there I saw a young French woman leave her house and pass him on the bridge. She was leaving the village for a safer place but she seemed quite composed and carried a basket on her left arm.

While our village was being destroyed we were startled by a tremendous explosion a few miles away; and looking to our left we saw a huge tongue of flame leap up to the sky, followed by a wonderful pillar of smoke which stood rigid for some moments like a monster tower of Babel reaching up to the heavens. Evidently a dump of cordite had been fired by an enemy shell. Farther off still, another dump was on fire. Time and again, bright flames leapt from the ground only to be smothered again by dense curling masses of smoke. It seemed as if our whole front was on fire, and news came to us that our main road of communication had been heavily shelled, and was now strewn with dead horses and men. Before the battle of the Somme there were no signs and portents so terrible as these: It was evident that the enemy knew what was in store for him on the morrow, and was preparing against it, but if the prelude was so magnificent in its terror, what would the battle be? Imagination staggered under the contemplation. By four o'clock the bombardment was almost at an end, and nearly all the shells in the Square had exploded. The soldiers began to creep out of the cellars. On passing through the Square we were amazed at the sight. In fact the Transport Officer passed through at my side without recognizing the place. At the entrance was a team of six dead mules lying prone on the ground and terribly torn. Two rows of houses had disappeared, leaving mere heaps of stones in their places. The pavement was torn up, and the wrecks of the ammunition wagons lay scattered about. Two houses were still burning.

Our colonel and adjutant we found by the side of the stream. They had been in a cellar near the Square all day but, fortunately, they were little the worse for the experience. They were giving orders for the assembling of the scattered regiment.

By this time, civilians were leaving the cellars, and with armfuls of household goods hastening from the village. To them it seemed the end of all things--the day of doom. Some of them had slight wounds and as they passed us they cried mournfully, "Finis, Messieurs, Finis." All was lost. This exodus of the despairing civilians was the saddest sight of the day. By sunset the regiment had been gathered together--all except the wounded who had been sent to the Main Dressing Station and the dead who had been placed side by side and covered with blankets. Most of our officers and men had lost all their belongings, but in the twilight they marched out of the village and took their places in the reserve trenches near the other battalions. These had suffered no losses. They had been saved the long day's agony. Early in the morning the battle was to begin but the Westminsters knew that no worse experience could await them than that through which they had already passed.

Next morning I buried, near the ruined church, the bodies of the sergeants who had been killed a few doors from us; and on the following day I laid to rest, side by side, in one long grave, two drivers who had died at their posts in the Square, together with an officer and twenty men belonging to the 1st Queen's Westminster Rifles.

VII
"NOW THE DAY IS OVER"

Achicourt is a little village about a mile out of Arras. It has two churches, one Roman Catholic, the other, Lutheran. The former church has been utterly destroyed by German shells, and will have to be rebuilt from the foundations. The Lutheran church was less prominently placed, and its four walls are still standing. Its humility has saved it, but, as by fire. All its windows are gone, and its walls are torn and scarred by fragments of shells. Most of its slates have been destroyed and the rain pours through the roof. But, on dry days, and until the Battle of Arras, it was a beloved little place for services. It stood, however, at a corner of the village Square, and the Square was destroyed by hundreds of exploding shells on Easter Sunday. As I passed it in the afternoon of that day, and saw how it had suffered, my heart grew sad within me.

Often it had sheltered us at worship, and many of our most sacred memories will, for ever, cling like ivy to its walls. The door was smashed in, the vestibule torn into strips as by lightning. The pews were strewn on the floor with their backs broken; even the frames of the windows had been blown out. There was a little portable organ that we had used with our hymns, and it lay mutilated on the floor like a slaughtered child. The floor was white with plaster, as when a sharp frost has brought low the cherry blossom. Never again, I thought, should I gather my men for worship within its humble, hospitable walls. One more of the beautiful and sacred things of life had perished in this all-devouring war. Only the fields remained, and there all my future services must be held.

But "fears may be liars" and so mine proved. I had reckoned without the man in khaki--that master of fate whose head "beneath the bludgeonings of chance, is bloody but unbowed." In a week he had cleared the Square of its dead--mules and men--filled in its craters, and cleared away the debris that blocked the roads. He was even removing the fallen houses in order to mend the roads with their bricks and stones; and he had thrown together all the scraps of iron for salvage. There I found, lying side by side, the burned tin-soldiers of the children; officers' revolvers which, being loaded, had exploded in the heat; bayonets and rifle-barrels of the men; broken sewing machines of the women. He had taken in hand, too, the little church. Sacking was spread across the windows; the remnants of the little organ were carefully placed under the pulpit where they lay like the body of a saint beneath an altar; the floor was swept of its fallen plaster. The pews were repaired and placed in order again, and a new door was made. Even timber was brought for a new vestibule. The wood was rough and unpainted--Tommy had to use what he could get--but it served. The twisted railings were drawn away from the entrance, and, on the following Sunday, we were back in our old sanctuary. We felt that it was more sacred than ever. These are the deeds of our fighting-man that make us love him so much, and these are the acts of kindness and common sense that make us admire our commanders. Both officers and men have the heart of a lion in the hour of battle, the gentleness of a lamb when it is over. Whatever their circumstances, they cannot cease to be gentlemen, nor forget the fathers that begat them.

Let him who doubts the future of England come hither. He will see the past through the present, and the future through both. Tommy's eyes are the crystal gazing-glasses in which he will discern the future. Tommy is living history and the prophecy of the future made flesh. The pessimists have not seen Tommy here, and that is why they are what they are. "Age cannot wither nor custom stale" his infinite freshness and resource. He is a sword that the rust of time cannot corrode, nor the might of an enemy break, and he will be found flashing wherever there are wrongs to right and weak to be defended. On Easter Sunday he was calmly enduring the horror of the German bombardment and the explosions of his own dump of shells. On Easter Monday he was driving the Germans at the point of his bayonet, or accepting their surrender at the doors of their dug-outs! On Easter Tuesday and Wednesday he was repairing a little French chapel for worship. Take him which day you will, and you will find him mighty hard to match. To me he is the king of men, and his genius, cheerfulness and resourcefulness beyond the range of explanations.

After some weeks of fighting we had come to our last Sunday in Achicourt, and were gathered for the evening service. The chapel was jammed with officers and men, but not all my flock was there. There was Rifleman Gibson absent. He was carrying his beloved Lewis gun in an attack when a bullet struck him, and he died, as his comrades report, with a smile upon his face. Before going into the battle he had given me his father's address and thanked me for the spiritual help he had received at the services. It was his farewell to me, and his father now has the penciled words. And Rifleman Stone was absent, too. He was but a boy, and beautiful with youth and goodness. His comrades loved him as David loved Jonathan, with a love passing the love of women. Every day, they told me in their grief, he knelt in the trench to say his prayers and to read his Bible. One night after praying he laid him down and slept. He had often sung the evening hymn:

"Jesus protects; my fears, be gone!

What can the Rock of Ages move?

Safe in Thy arm I lay me down,

Thy everlasting arms of love.

"While Thou art intimately nigh,

Who, then, shall violate my rest?

Sin, earth, and hell I now defy;

I lean upon my Saviour's breast.

"Me for Thine own Thou lov'st to take,

In time and in eternity,

Thou never, never wilt forsake

A helpless soul that trusts in Thee."

And as he slept, God took him from the misery of this world--took him without waking him. His broken-hearted comrades gathered together his broken body, and a friend, a Congregational preacher, who, though over military age, was serving in the ranks, read the burial service over him. Lance-corporal Gilbert James was missing, too--he whom I had known to lose his breakfast to attend a service in a cold, dirty, old barn. And many others were absent whose departure to the Land beyond our mortal reach was to us like the putting out of stars.

We were leaving the Arras front and we sang a hymn for those who had taken our places:

"O Lord of Hosts, Whose mighty arm

In safety keeps 'mid war's alarm,

Protect our comrades at the Front

Who bear of war the bitter brunt.

And in the hour of danger spread

Thy sheltering wings above each head,

"In battle's harsh and dreadful hour,

Make bare Thine arm of sovereign power,

And fight for them who fight for Thee,
And give to justice, victory.
O in the hour of danger spread
Thy sheltering wings above each head.

"If by the way they wounded lie,
O listen to their plaintive cry;
And rest them on Thy loving breast,
O Thou on Whom the cross was pressed;
And in the hour of danger shed
Thy glorious radiance o'er each head.

"When pestilence at noonday wastes,
And death in triumph onward hastes,
O Saviour Christ, remember Nain,
And give us our beloved again.
In every ward of sickness tread,
And lay Thy hand upon each head.

"O Friend and Comforter divine,
Who makest light at midnight shine,
Give consolation to the sad
Who in the days of peace were glad.
And in the hour of sorrow spread
Thy wings above each drooping head.
Amen."

I had to find a new voice to start it, for our little organ had been destroyed by a shell, and our precentor was lying in a grave beside his Medical Aid Post at Guemappe. When, on Good Friday, we had sung the hymn before, the regiment returned from rest billets to the line, he had started the tune. His love for music was second only to that of risking his life for the wounded. In one of his letters given me to censor, he had written, "How nice it will be to be back in my old place in the choir." But he was destined not to go back. His path was onward and upward, and his place was in the heavenly choir. I had seen it in his large, tender blue eyes. There was in them an expression as if he had seen "the land that is very far off." I felt that he was chosen as a sacrifice--that the seal of God was on his forehead.

Still, we had to sing, though his voice was silent. So we sang--several tunes, for hymns seemed all our spirits needed. What need was there for a sermon when we had hymns? We left the rag-time type of hymn and sang the real deep things that come from men's hearts, and ever after are taken up by their fellows to express their deepest aspirations and experiences. The ruined chapel vibrated with music, and men, I am told, stood in the street to listen while "Jesus, Lover of my Soul," "Rock of Ages," "When I Survey the Wondrous Cross" and "The Sands of Time are Sinking" told of the faith and love that lift up the heart. We also sang "Abide with Me." After hearing us sing it one night, a Roman Catholic officer in the regiment, a Canadian and one of the bravest, most beloved men that ever walked, told me that he was a great-grandson of the author. He is in hospital now with severe wounds, but his men were present.

"Couldn't we take up a collection for the repair of the chapel when peace comes?" whispered a rifleman; "it would be a sort of thanksgiving for the good times we have had in it, and for the kindness of the congregation in giving us the use of it so freely."

I put the suggestion to the men and they voted for it with enthusiasm. Two of them went round with their caps and out of their shallow purses the big-hearted fellows gave over 100 francs. In the name of the men I presented the full caps to a lady of the congregation who was present, and she was moved to tears. The time was quickly passing, so I mounted the pulpit and told them of words spoken after the earth's first great trouble, when the black wings of death had cast their shadow over every home: "And God said, I do set my bow in the cloud, and it shall be for a token of a covenant between me and the earth. And it shall come to pass, when I bring a cloud over the earth, that the bow shall be seen in the cloud."

"God," I said, "has made a covenant with man, for man is His neighbor and subject; and there must be an understanding between them, if there is to be peace and happiness. Man must know God's will or he will grieve Him and there will be discord and pain. Also, man must know God's intentions concerning him, and something of His ways, or else he will live in fear and dread of the Almighty One in whose power he lies. There were no books and parchment in the first days, so God took the sky for His parchment, and dipping His fingers in the most lovely of colors, wrote out

His covenant with man. He spread it out between earth and heaven so that man might look up and see it without obstruction, and so that He Himself might look down on it and remember His agreement. 'The bow,' He said, 'shall be in the cloud; and I will look upon it, that I may remember the everlasting covenant.'"

"When you draw up a covenant with a neighbor, you look well at it and then give it to your attorney, who puts it away in the darkness of the safe. But it is taken out at intervals for fresh examination. And the rainbow-covenant was put away behind the clouds, to be brought out again from time to time to bring comfort and strength to man by its appearance. The rainbow is only half seen by man. The lower half of its circle is lost in the earth. It exists, but unseen. And the full circle of God's beautiful covenant with man has never appeared to our eyes. A full half is lost in the unapprehending darkness of man's mind. The full purpose of God is not realized. His plans are too vast and glorious for the intellect or imagination to span; but half the rainbow is seen and it is enough. Seeing half we can take the rest on trust. In the covenant we are assured that we shall never be given darkness without light, winter without summer, seedtime without harvest, death without birth, sorrow without joy, or a thick cloud without a rainbow. He binds Himself not to give evil without good, or to bring tears without laughter. "I do set My bow in the cloud; and it shall come to pass when I bring a cloud over the earth, that the bow shall be seen in the cloud."

"A rainbow is made up of rain and sunshine and life is woven of the same stuff--tears and laughter. The most glorious sunshine is incapable of a rainbow without the co-operation of the dark trailing clouds; and it is impossible for the human character to reach its ripest maturity and beauty on joy alone. Sorrow is as beneficent and necessary as joy. There are untutored natives who dread the rainbow. They believe that it is a serpent that rises out of the pools to devour men; and there are unbelieving men in cultured lands who dread adversity no less. They do not believe that *God* 'brings the cloud.' The rainbow is their refutation and it is written across the sky for all to see. On the other hand, there are unbelieving men who see only the cloud and are blind to the sunshine. To them life is one long tragedy. It is an immense futility. They regard man as a mere cork in the sea, thrown about by blind, deaf, unintelligible natural forces void of purpose; active indeed but ungoverned. Human life to them is a black cloud driven through immensity by the winds of unintelligent fate. It has no meaning and its darkness is the deeper because they cannot call a halt and disperse it into nothingness. Like Job's wife they would say 'Curse God and die,' yet they cannot die. But Job, as he sits on the dunghill, looks up at the rainbow and finds a truer philosophy. 'What?' says he, 'shall we receive good at the hand of God, and shall we not receive evil?' Under the rainbow's arch there are fruitful fields and beautiful gardens for where the rainbow hangs in air there is sunshine and there is rain--the parents of fruitfulness. And to whom God gives in equal measure joy and sorrow there is beauty and fruitfulness of heart and life. His promise to 'every living creature' is that He will never send the cloud without the sunshine and, what is not less gracious, He will never send the sunshine without the cloud. When by day the Israelites tramped the fiery desert He led them by a pillar of cloud, and they marched in its shade; and in the blackness of night He threw in the sky a pillar of sunshine; and they walked through the gloom in its light.

"In these terrible days of war when our hearts begin to fail us and dark doubts cloud the mind, let us look at the Covenant God has made with us. He has set it in rainbow colors across the sky, that 'he who runs may read' and 'the wayfaring man though a fool may not err.' God has flung his rainbow over the trench and the grave; over the Garden of Gethsemane; over the Cross on Calvary. It is over the tomb in the Arimathean's Garden; and over Olivet, as Christ ascends to heaven. We are born under the rainbow, live under it, die under it. At the last we shall find it over the throne of Judgment. Water and blood flowed from Christ's side; and life and death, joy and pain, light and darkness, summer and winter, peace and war come forth from God.

"Let us take life as it comes with obedient wills and grateful hearts. The bee finds honey in the thistle as well as in the rose, and 'where the bee sucks there suck I,' for He who guides the bee guides me. Only in loving obedience to God shall we find true wisdom. It is not so much what we are given as how we take it that matters. To be humble nothing may be so sweet as sorrow; and to the proud nothing may be so bitter as pleasure. Let us leave God to mix the ingredients of our life, for 'all things work together for good to them that love God.' It is all in the covenant written by God's fingers in the colors of the rainbow, and whenever He brings it from beyond the clouds, let us look at it with reverent eyes, and ponder its promise. Then shall we be able to say, with Wordsworth,

'My heart leaps up when I behold

A rainbow in the sky.'"

After I had finished speaking we sang, at the request of one of the sergeants, the hymn commencing

"The Day Thou gavest Lord is ended,

The darkness falls at Thy behest."

And beautiful indeed was the singing of it.

The Benediction followed. Just as I was ending it an impulse came to me, and I yielded to its importunity. "Before we part and before we leave Achicourt which has meant so much to us of joy and sorrow," I said, "let us sing a kiddies' hymn. We still shelter in our hearts a little child. Though we have grown moustaches and some of us gray hairs, the child that we once were, never quite dies. Let us have a hymn for the boy within us who never grows up and never dies." Then I read out verse by verse, for it was not in their books:

"Now the day is over,

Night is drawing nigh,

Shadows of the evening

Steal across the sky.

"Jesus, give the weary

Calm and sweet repose;

With Thy tenderest blessing

May their eyelids close.

"Grant to little children

Visions bright of Thee;

Guarding the sailors tossing

On the angry sea.

"Comfort every sufferer

Watching late in pain;

Those who plan some evil

From their sin restrain.

"When the morning wakens,

Then may I arise

Pure and fresh, and sinless

In Thy holy eyes."

I have witnessed many moving sights in my time and heard much deep and thrilling music; but I have never been so deeply moved by anything as by the rich, deep voices of these gallant men and boys who, after winning the Battle of Arras, had come into this ruined church and were singing this beautiful kiddies' hymn as their last farewell.

The collection the boys had taken up had been so heavy that we carried it to the French lady's house for her. As we entered her home she said in her simple way, as her eyes grew radiant with gratitude, "I like the English soldiers." It was the voice of France. And she was worthy to speak for France. For two-and-a-half years her house had stood within a mile of the German trenches, and but a few hundred yards from our own firing line. Yet she and her mother had never left it. She introduced me to her mother, who had lived in London, and spoke English. Then she brought in coffee. I had noticed a most remarkable thing about the house. There was not a piece of glass broken, nor a mark of war on the walls. It was the only house I have seen, either in Achicourt or Arras, upon which the war has not laid its monstrous and bloody finger. "How is it," I asked the mother, "that your house has not been touched?" Her eyes shone and a sweet smile lit up her face. "It is the will of God," she said simply. "Shells have fallen a little short of us and a little beyond us. They have passed within a yard of the house, and we have heard the rushing of the wind as they passed, but they have not touched us. When the village has been bombarded we have gone down into the cellar as was but discretion and duty, but we have had the conviction all along that we should be spared, and we refused to leave the house. We do not know God's purpose but we believe that it is God's will to spare us." I leave the fact to speak for itself and offer no explanation. Skeptics will say the house was spared by accident; but they would not have stayed there two-and-a-half years trusting to such an accident. These two women, without a man in the house, stayed on the very confines of hell with its hourly suspense and danger for nearly three years, because they believed it was God's will and that, though they walked through the fiery furnace heated seven times hotter than it was wont to be heated, He would not allow so much as a hair of their heads to be singed. And not a hair was singed. They were women in whom faith burned like a bright pillar of fire. One caught its light, and felt its heat. I have met patriots and heroes and know their quality when I see them and come near them. These were "the real thing." Faith in God and faith in their country were interwoven in their spirits like sun and shower in a rainbow. They were of the same breed as the Maid of France, and like her, with their white banner bearing the device of the Cross, they withstood and defied the might and terror of the invader. They believed it was God's will they should stay, to "Be still and know that I am God." Their experience was expressed by the Psalmist centuries ago: "God is our refuge and strength, a very present help in trouble. Therefore will not we fear, though the earth be removed, and though the mountains be carried into the midst of the sea. Though the waters thereof roar and be troubled, though the mountains shake with the swellings thereof ... Come behold the works of the Lord, what desolations He hath made in the earth. He maketh wars to cease unto the end of the earth; He breaketh the bow, and cutteth the spear in sunder; He burneth the chariot in the fire.... The Lord of Hosts is with us; the God of Jacob is our refuge."

Such was the faith of these two women, and their courage few men have approached. It is a practical matter, and after comparing it with the skeptic's theory of accident and coincidence and remembering his probable haste in seeking a place not so liable to untoward accidents, I accept the explanation of the women. Their house was spared and not a hair of their heads injured because "it was God's will." If it is not the correct theory, it ought to be. Otherwise falsehood is more sustaining than truth, and inspires nobler conduct.

The day was now over. A new chapter of life had been written, and in the morning, we left behind us this village of precious memories, and marched out again into the unknown.

VIII
SONS OF THE MOTHERLAND

It is said that the eel is born in the deepest part of the ocean, thousands of miles from any country, and that, urged by an overpowering instinct it begins almost at once to rise towards the light and to head for the land. After slowly swimming thousands of miles it reaches our rivers, and pushes its way up to their sources, and even crawls through the grass out of one stream into another. Here, if uncaught by man, it lives for years gorging an appetite which only developed on reaching the fresh water. Then, the overmastering instinct that brought it out, takes it back. It returns through the illimitable waters until it finds the place where it was born. There the female lays her eggs and there male and female die. The eggs hatch, and the young do as their parents did before them.

I do not think I could kill or eat an eel. I have too much reverence for it now that I have learned its story. When in the fish market I see an eel struggling, I feel that I want to take it and drop it into the sea that it may go to its long home "far from the madding crowd's ignoble strife." How passionate and wild must be its desire to get back to its own ocean depths where it may perpetuate its kind and die in peace. Its appetite is voracious, but then, what but the mightiest and most elemental instincts and appetites could carry it through achievements so sublime and tragic. Picture it on its lone way through the deep, urged on by it knows not what. Scientists say that man has evolved from a tiny form of life that passed through the fish stage. If so, it explains a lot and I, for one, shall not be ashamed to acknowledge relationship to a fish with a life story as sublime as that of the eel. I know that Genesis speaks truly when it says that God made us out of the dust of the earth and breathed into our souls the breath of His own being thus animating dust with divinity. And if from the other inspired book, the book of Nature, scientists can teach how God mixed the clay when He fashioned man I will accept the teaching with gratitude, for it will help me to understand things that are dark in me and in my fellows. It will throw light on the wild longings, and instincts immature, that baffle the mind, and come into the clear shallow streams of life like eels out of the dark unfathomable depths of the ocean.

Since I went to France I have been amazed at the homing instinct as revealed in the coming together of the sons of the British Motherland. People at home do not quite realize what has happened. Britain's sons have come back to her--have come back to die that their race may be saved and perpetuated. The British are a roving race. A large number of them yield to an overpowering desire to go out into the world. The South Pole and the North Pole have known the tread of their feet. Their ships have anchored in every creek of every sea. There is no town or country however remote where their voices have not been heard. Even Mecca could not keep the Briton out. He must look upon its Black Stone. All lands call him to come, and see, and conquer. He colonizes and absorbs but cannot be absorbed. He is a Briton still. A friend of mine told me that when visiting Australia strangers who had never seen England, except in and through their fathers, would come to him in railway carriage or 'bus, and ask "How is everything at *Home*?" And Dr. Fitchett, Australia's splendid author, confesses that when he first saw the land of his fathers he knelt down and kissed its shore.

Loving the homeland with a passion stronger than death the Briton leaves it, for he hears the call of the world borne on the winds and waves from afar, and cannot refuse it. In foreign lands he lives and labors. He roams their fields and swims in their streams, but always with an ear listening for the voice of the Motherland; for he is hers, and at her service if she calls.

The Declaration of War on Aug. 4, 1914, was the Mother's call to her children. Swifter than lightning it passed through the waves and on the wings of the wind. The settler left his lonely cabin, the gold-digger his shovel, the prospector his surveying instruments, the rancher his herds, the missionary his church, the teacher his school, the clerk his office, and all made for the nearest port. Within a month there was not a ship on the wide seas but was bearing loyal sons back to their Motherland's defense. I have met, in France, British soldiers from every country under heaven. I bent over a dying soldier near Arras who was a clerk in Riga, Russia, when the call came. And one night on the Somme a fine young fellow from Africa entered my tent, and slept by my side. He was one of the most charming and handsome men I have ever met, and had come from Durban. He had fought with Botha in Southwest Africa, and at the conclusion of that campaign had shipped for home. Next day I took him to Delville Wood for he wanted to see the place where his brother had died. I found that he was of my own communion and we talked about some of my college friends who had gone out to Natal. Two days later, he died of wounds in a dressing station. Most of the transport officers in our Division have come home from abroad, and have been given their posts because they are accustomed to horses. One was prospecting in Nigeria, another salmon-canning in Siberia, a third on a plantation in South America.

In addition to Canadians, South Africans, Australians, and New Zealanders, who have come by the hundred thousand at the call of the Motherland, there are hundreds of thousands who have come singly, or in small parties, from remote corners of the earth. For five weeks I was a patient in a Canadian hospital in France. The entire staff was Canadian. Some were

Canadian born; others had gone out to that country years ago. All were of British blood. The colonel was a magnificent specimen of manhood from London, Ontario, in which city he had been born. He would sit on the bed and tell us tales of the great snow-land. Sometimes he would scold us for being so blind to the greatness of the Empire and tell us what Canada thought of the Motherland. One of the night orderlies would, on occasion, recite to us some poem such as "Jim Bludso," before the lights went out. Then he would come to my locker and take "Palgrave's Treasury of Songs and Lyrics" with which to regale his soul during the long watches of the night. He was of the full stature of men and straight as a pine. He had gone out from Ireland as a boy, and settled on a cattle ranch in the United States. One day there was trouble and one of the other cowboys sent a bullet clean through his chest. The moment war was declared he left his roving herds of cattle, crossed the frontier into Canada and traveled hundreds of miles to Winnipeg to enlist. The doctor looked at him. "What is this scar on your chest?" he asked. "Oh," replied the cowboy, "I fell off a wagon and knocked the skin off." The doctor turned him round and put his finger in the scar on his back where the bullet had passed out. "And what is this scar at the back? Did you fall off another wagon?" And the two men understood one another and laughed. The doctor could not find it in his heart to send the cowboy back to his ranch, so he was passed into the Canadian contingent.

One of the nurses we called "the Little Mother." She had gone to Canada five years before, but the war had brought her back, and well was it for us that it had. Among the patients was a doctor in the American A.M.C. His ancestors had left England generations ago and settled in New England, but he had come back at the call of war--a grandson of the Motherland. Then there was a lieutenant of British stock who had been born and brought up at Antwerp, but as the German guns were destroying his native city he took ship to enlist in the British army. "Anzac" was, as his nickname denotes, an Australian. He was in the Flying Corps. He had heard the call at school and had come "home" to the land of his fathers.

In one regiment I found a bunch of lads who had been born in China. But, out there in Hong Kong, they heard the call of a Motherland they had never seen, and came post haste to her help. Sitting near me as I write, is an officer back from the Argentine, and already, on his arm, is a gold wound-stripe. Another in the mess had been pearl-fishing in Australia, but stored his boats to come and fight. Another at our table was born in Australia. He was with Captain Falcon Scott on his last expedition, and saw him go out to the South Pole and death. He has already been wounded. When the war broke out its tumult seemed to wake our fathers and we felt them stir in our blood; for ancestors are not put into graves but are buried alive in their sons. We felt the call to defend our race as our fathers did in their day. It was a master instinct, and the millions of men who voluntarily left home and business to fight show how deeply nationality is rooted in human nature. Returning from a far land to die--if needs be--that their kind may live, the scattered sons of our Motherland have come by all the seas to defend her, in her hour of need.

"They came as the winds come

When forests are rended;

They came as the waves come

When navies are stranded."

IX
THE TERROR BY NIGHT

June was a flaming month on the high ground we had captured beyond Arras. The Quartermaster and Transport Officer with whom I was messing were both "on leave" so, as I was the only officer left in the camp, a Baptist padre, whose regiment was near, came to live with me. I had a little brown tent five feet wide and six feet long which a rifleman had lent to me because the bell-tent I was expecting had not arrived. The rifleman did not need his tent, for he and his chums had built themselves a little dug-out. Next day the bell-tent arrived, and the other padre took possession of it, while I held on to the little brown shelter. Next to it was the kitchen where the servants slept and cooked. It was a truly wonderful contrivance of wood, corrugated iron and ground-sheets. The Baptist chaplain's tent was round, my shelter oblong, but what shape the kitchen was, would pass the wit of man to say. It was a shape never seen on earth before. It had no ancestor and it could have no descendant. Such a design could not occur twice. Beyond the kitchen were the horse-lines of the regiment and close by them the regimental stores. It was so hot that we all wore our lightest clothing; and when the servants got lemons from Arras, the lemonade they made lasted about five minutes only, for what was left by us was quickly drunk up by the servants with the assistance of those who like to frequent such happy places as mess kitchens.

All our meals were served out of doors, under the blue sky. We had guests most days, for officers coming out from the homeland stayed with us for a night or a day before going up with the rations to join the regiment in the trench. Other officers had come down to stay with us on their way to a course at some military school; and one, at least, came to wait for the day on which he was to take his "leave." We were, therefore, a very merry party. It was almost like camping on the Yorkshire moors, for we had an uninterrupted view of many miles. To those who love vast stretches of wild barren country as I do, the scene under the flaming June sun was exceedingly impressive. There were no houses, streams, hedges, or trees, but the whole area was scored with trenches cut into the white chalk, and showing clearly at great distances. The ground, with but short spaces between, was covered with encampments. These consisted of the stores and horse-lines of the regiments and batteries in the line. The circle of the horizon was bounded by the charred ruins of French villages--Beaurains, Neuville, Vitasse, Wancourt, Monchy and Tilloy. We could see the flashing of our own guns, and the black bursts of shells from those of the enemy.

All day the sky was thick with aeroplanes, and many were too high to be seen except through strong field glasses. We watched a German aeroplane circling over Arras and directing the fire of the long guns. Soon the streets were strewn with dead and wounded, for the town was full of troops. The firing only lasted a few minutes, however. One of our aeroplanes quickly challenged the enemy to single combat; and we soon saw the German machine falling from an immense height, wing over wing and head over tail, utterly out of control.

Dinner, in the cool of the evening, was a most pleasant meal. As we drank our coffee we watched the aeroplanes returning from the line like birds to their nests. Sometimes we counted as many as twenty, all heading for home at the same time. The sun set in red and golden splendor, and we wondered what darkness would bring. On the night before our arrival, the regiment which made way for us had one of its storemen killed by a shell; and on most nights a few shells fell in some part or other of the vast camp. One evening shells fell a little beyond us and the transport-sergeant moved his horse-lines. After that, he moved them every evening at dark, so that the ground where the enemy had observed the horses in the day-time was left vacant when he opened fire at night. It was a game of chess with horses and men for pawns, and life and death for the stakes.

On the evening before, our guest--a young lieutenant--was to go on leave, he got very uneasy. As gulls scent the approach of stormy weather and come inland, or blackbirds and larks feel the approach of winter and migrate to summer lands, so men can sometimes scent danger and coming death. He had with him a bottle of whisky, and he kept it on the table outside my tent--a safe place for it.

"I don't mind telling you, Padre," he said, as he poured out a glass, "I've got the 'wind-up' badly to-night. I don't like the feel of things. I would rather be in the trenches than here, because I know what is likely to happen there, but here in the open I feel strange and unprotected. I shall be glad when it is morning."

His feeling was quite natural. We always feel another man's dangers more than our own because they are new to us and we don't know what to expect or how to meet them. A man will choose a big danger that he is used to, sooner than a lesser danger that is new to him. Besides, the lieutenant had his "leave-warrant" in his breast pocket and that will sap any man's courage. He has a feeling that the shells are after his "leave-warrant" and that the gunners know where it is. He suspects that fate is malignant and takes a special delight in killing a man when he is on the way to "Blighty." Many a man has been killed with a "leave-warrant" in his pocket, or "commission papers" in it which were taking him home.

Our doctor told me how one night he and the chaplain who preceded me were riding on the front of an ambulance car when a shell burst and with a fragment killed the chaplain. In the padre's pocket was his warrant, and he was taking his last ride before going home; but instead of going home in "Blighty" he went to his *long* home, and the warrant lies in the grave with him. A man feels particularly vulnerable when the long-looked-for "leave-warrant" is in his pocket. He does not fear death after "leave," but he does on the eve of "leave." He wants one more look at his home and loved ones before going on the long and lone journey which, despite all the comfort which the Christian religion gives, still retains much of its terror to the human spirit. There have been few better Christians than Samuel Johnson and John Bunyan, but neither of them could contemplate fording the river of death without misgivings. When they came to it they found it much less formidable than they had expected. Had they been at the Front with "leave-warrants" in their pockets to "Fleet Street, London," or "Elstow, Bedford," I fancy neither of them would have taken undue risks.

I could sympathize with the young lieutenant for, a few months before, a "leave-warrant" had made a bit of a coward of myself. I was in two minds whether or not to go up to the firing line to see the men again before shipping for home. The "leave-warrant" was in my pocket, and I was to go next morning; but the doctor's story of my predecessor came to my mind, and the "leave-warrant" spread itself out before the eyes of my imagination. I saw the faces of my wife, and mother, and dog, and the faces of my friends. The old home and the green fields stretched out before me; and I decided to see them first and the "boys" after. I had just been with my men, but it was a long time since I had been with those at home. If there was a shell with my name and address on it, I thought I would make the Hun wait till I had been home, before I let him deliver it into my hands. I think a "leave-warrant" would make a coward of any man. At any rate, the feeling is quite understood and recognized by everyone at the Front; and this young officer had been sent down from the trenches to us, three days before his train was due to start, so that he might have a better chance of using his "warrant," and at the same time, feel more at ease in mind.

I undressed and got into bed, and lay reading by the light of a candle when the lieutenant came to the tent door again. "It's no use, Padre," he said, "I can't go to bed yet. I feel too uneasy. I wish I were on the train." He went back to the bell-tent he was sharing with the other chaplain, and I put out my light.

There was the silence of a summer evening broken only by the distant bursting of shells. Then, suddenly, there was a crash about seventy yards from our tents, and two more near the horse-lines. "To run or not run?" that was the question; and my answer was in the negative. If I ran, it was just as likely that I should run into a shell, as out of the way of one. On Easter Sunday I had seen three of our non-commissioned officers killed in that way. Besides, I like my bed, once I have taken the trouble to get into it. I therefore put on my steel helmet which I had placed by the bed-side, and waited to see what would happen. (A steel helmet is a wonderful comfort when men are under fire. We may not have much in our heads but we feel more anxious about them than about all the rest of the body. The helmets are heavy and uncomfortable and we don't like wearing them, but, nevertheless, may blessings ever rest on the head of the man who invented them. I have seen scores of lives saved by them, and they have given infinite comfort and assurance in trying moments.)

A long silence elapsed, then the lieutenant appeared at the door of the tent again.

"You haven't been here all the time, have you?" he asked. "We went down to the old trenches at the bottom of the camp; but it is rather cold and wearisome there, and I think the worst is over now. I'm just going to take another sip of the 'Scotch wine' and then turn in for the night; but I'm not going to undress."

Ten minutes later there was a tremendous crash as if a star had fallen on top of us. There came a blinding flash of light, a strong smell of powder, and a spluttering of bullets on the ground. That was enough to get the laziest man living out of bed, and to answer the question, "to run or not to run?" in the affirmative. I slipped on my boots without fastening them, put on my trench coat and bade my little tent a fond farewell. There were some old German gun-pits close by, and I sought refuge there. "Come in here, sir," cried a voice, and I found myself by the side of a sergeant. Then the cook ran in bare-foot and laughing. No one seemed to have been hit, and all had now sought shelter. We waited for some time and nothing further happened. The night was cold and I began to shiver in my pajamas. So I started to look about for a place to sleep in, for a feeling of estrangement had grown up between me and the little brown tent. There was a path across a shallow bit of trench, and underneath it I found the barber, lying comfortably on his bed. He invited me in, and said that I could have the bed, and he would sleep at the side of it on his ground-sheet. He could, he said, sleep as soundly on the ground as on the bed of stretched sacking. I therefore returned to my tent to get blankets. The time-fuse of a shell had gone through the kitchen and rebounded from a beam on to my servant, but without doing him any injury and he proposed sleeping there for the night. He only agreed to move to some safer place, when I ordered him to do so. There was no one in the bell-tent so I knew the occupants were quite safe somewhere. On striking a light to get my blankets, I noticed three small holes in the top of the tent, and knew that shrapnel bullets had missed me only by inches. It had been a close shave and it was not inappropriate that I was now going to be the guest of a barber.

The psychological effect was not one I should have expected. The incident caused no shell-shock, and but little immediate excitement; so I was soon asleep. All the others were in a like case. The excitement came with the morning when we examined the tents and the ground. In the bell-tent there were ten shrapnel bullet holes. One had gone through the piece of wood on which the officers' clothing had been hung, and must have passed immediately over the body of the Baptist chaplain as he lay in bed. Others must have passed equally near the lieutenant who was not in bed, but, standing up at the time, fully dressed. In my own little tent I found eleven holes and they were in all parts of the canvas. Some of the bullets must have gone in at one side and out at the other, for only five were found embedded in the hard, chalky ground. A sixth had passed through the box at the bed-head and entered deeply into the book I had been reading. Outside the kitchen, the servants picked up a lump of shell a foot long and three or four inches wide. Well was it for them that the fragment fell outside the kitchen and not inside. The ground around the tents was sprinkled with shrapnel bullets and bits of shell. The shells which fell near the horses had burst on touching the ground, and not like ours, in the air. They had dug deep holes in the earth, and as the horses were within a few yards of them, it seemed miraculous that none was hurt. The transport had just returned from taking up the rations, and, as one of the drivers leapt off his horse, a bullet hit the saddle where his leg had been a second before. Not a man or horse received a scratch, although the shells had made a direct hit on our camp. On other occasions one shell has laid out scores of men and horses.

They say that sailors don't like padres on board ship, because they think the latter bring them bad luck. And most people are a little afraid of the figure thirteen, but though it was the thirteenth of June and there were two padres in the tents, we had the best of what is called "luck." So I think we may say it was one up for the padres. After breakfast we gathered together some of the fragments lying around the tents, and found the nose-cap of a shell which had burst seventy yards away. With these, and the time-fuse which hit my servant, the other chaplain and I went to a battery and asked the officers to tell us something about the gun, just as one might take a bone of some extinct creature to a scientist, and ask him to draw an outline of the whole animal. They told us that the gun was a long-range, high-velocity, naval gun with a possible range of fifteen miles. They knew where it was, but could not hit it. The shot was a large high-explosive, shrapnel shell, and the time-fuse indicated that it had come to us from about eleven miles away.

On our return we built ourselves dug-outs for the nights, and only lived in the tents by day. Sometimes we were shelled in the day-time, but by taking cover took no hurt, though a lad in the transport next to us was seriously wounded. When they were shelling us by day, we could distinctly hear the report of the gun, a second or two later, see the shell burst in the air; and a second later still, we could hear it. We saw the burst before we heard it.

I have given this personal incident not, I hope, out of any impulse of egotism, but because it furnishes those who have not been at the Front with an idea of the terror which assails our men by night, both in the trenches and in the "back areas." There can be but few who, having been any length of time at the Front, have not had similar experiences and equally narrow escapes. They are so common that men get used to them and do not take nearly enough care to protect themselves. Loss by such stray shells is expected, and the soldiers regard it much as a tradesman regards the deterioration of his stock. One gets used to the frequent occurrence of death as he does to anything else. At home there are thousands of preventable deaths--deaths through street accidents, diseases and underfeeding. The number could be enormously reduced if the nation would rouse itself. And human nature is much the same at the Front. Men prefer ease and comfort to safety. Also, men grow fatalistic. They have seen men sought out by shells after they have taken every precaution to escape them; and they have seen others go untouched when they seemed to be inviting shells to destroy them. Men are conscious of a Power that is not themselves directing their lives. They feel that in life which the Greek tragedians called Fate. They do not know quite what to call it. Most of them would call it Providence if they spoke frankly and gave it a name at all. One of the finest Christian officers I know told me that he believed that God's finger had already written what his fate should be. If he had to die nothing could save him, and if he had to live, nothing could kill him. All he was concerned with was to be able to do his duty, and take whatever God sent him. This, he said, was the only suitable working philosophy for a man at the Front.

There is a widespread fatalism at the Front, but it is the fatalism of Christ rather than of old Omar Khayyam: "Take no thought for your life ... for your heavenly Father knoweth that ye have need of all these things, but seek ye first the kingdom of God, and his righteousness. Take therefore no thought for the morrow; for the morrow shall take thought for the things of itself. Sufficient unto the day is the evil thereof." And this works. It enables men to "put a cheerful courage on" and do their duty. There is none of the paralysis of will and cessation of effort which follows the fatalistic philosophy of the East. All that Omar Khayyam's fatalism leaves a man to strive after is "Red, Red Wine," in which he drowns memory, honor and reputation and character. When he has passed from among his peers, there is nothing left to remember him by but a "turned-down empty glass." The Christian fatalism at the Front destroys no man's initiative, but keeps him merry and bright, and helps him to "do his bit." When he shall pass from the banqueting-house of life, into the Great Unexplored, he will leave as his memorial, not a turned-down glass, but a world redeemed from tyranny and wrong.

X
"ETON BOYS NEVER DUCK!"

An army is more courageous than the individuals who compose it. The coward finds sufficient courage for his job while doing it with his regiment, and the brave is at his bravest. He has a courage which is not his own but which, somehow, he puts on with his uniform. He does deeds of daring he could not have done as a civilian. The army has a corporate courage and each soldier receives a portion of it just as he receives a ration of the army's food. It is added to what he has of his own.

The badge of the army is courage. When a recruit joins the army he knows that he is putting away the civilian standard of courage with his derby hat, and is putting on the soldier's standard of courage with his uniform. His great fear is that he will not be able to live up to it. He wonders if he is made of the stuff that produces heroes. He is a mystery to himself and has a haunting fear that there may be a strain of the coward in his make-up. He wishes it were possible to have a rehearsal for he would rather die than fail on the appointed day.

The chaplain fears that he will faint and become a hindrance instead of a help when he first sees blood and torn limbs in the dressing station; and the recruit is afraid of being afraid in the hour of battle and of bringing dishonor and weakness upon his regiment. He will be glad when the trial is over--when he knows the stuff of which nature has made him. A friend of mine told me one day that he was walking over a heavily shelled field with a young aristocrat of a highly strung temperament. The man was afraid, but would not yield to his fear. His lips twitched and his face became drawn and white. His movements were jerky but he made no other sign. He talked about paltry things in which, at the moment, he had not the slightest interest, and passed jocular or sardonic remarks about the things that were happening around them. My friend ducked his head when a shell burst near as we all have done often enough, but the young aristocrat kept his head as high and stiff as if he were being crowned. He held it up defiantly; was it not filled with the bluest blood of England? The shells might blow it off if they liked. That was their concern, not his, but they should never make him bow. His fathers had fought on British battlefields for centuries, and had never bowed their heads to a foe, and he would not break the great tradition. Shells might break his neck but they should never bend it. He would face the enemy with as stiff an upper-lip and as stiff a neck as ever his fathers did. He knew his personal weakness and reinforced his strength with that of his fathers'. He was not afraid of death. He was afraid of being afraid.

My friend was a coachman's son who by courage and capacity of the highest order had won a commission. He had no traditions either to haunt or help him, and he had often been tried in the fire and knew his strength. He was not afraid of being afraid. It was natural to duck when a shell burst near and it did him no harm and made no difference to the performance of his duties; so he ducked as he felt inclined, and then laughed at his nerves for the tricks they were allowing the shells to play on them. But, knowing his companion's more sensitive nature and temperamental weakness, he was immensely impressed by his stiff neck and proudly erect head. He showed a self-control which only centuries of breeding could give. Here was a hero indeed. The shells he was defying were as nothing to the fears which haunted his imaginative nature and which, with his back to the wall of his family traditions, he was fighting and keeping at bay. My friend could not refrain from complimenting him on resisting the natural tendency to duck the head when a shell screamed above them.

"Eton boys never duck," replied the young aristocrat.

He was an Eton boy and would die rather than fall short of the Eton standard. In this war hundreds of them have died rather than save themselves by something which did not measure up to the Eton standard. The ranks of young British aristocrats have been terribly thinned in this war and I have heard their deeds spoken of with a reverence such as is only given to legendary heroes. They have gone sauntering over the crater-fields to their deaths with the same self-mastery and outward calm which the French aristocracy manifested as they mounted the steps of the guillotine in the Reign of Terror. To their own personal courage was added the courage of their race, and the accumulation of the centuries.

We speak of our new armies. There can be no "new" armies of Britons. The tradition of our newest army goes back to Boadicea. Its forerunners, without shields or armor, and almost without weapons, dared the Romans-- the proud conquerors of the world--to battle; and gave them the longest odds warriors ever gave. They knew they could not win but they knew they could die. Dead warriors they might become but never living slaves. They ran up Boadicea's proud banner because they knew that while the Romans might soak it in British blood, no power on earth could drag it through the mire.

Our forefathers crossed swords with Cæsar and his Roman legions, and our newest army goes into battle with the prestige born of two thousand years of war. They have a morale that belongs to the race in addition to the morale they possess as individuals. It is said that "the British do not know when they are beaten." How should they know? They have had no teachers. All they know is that if they have not gained the victory the battle is not ended and must go on until they pitch their tents on the undisputed field. The German Emperor spreads out his War Map but it is as undecipherable as the mountains in the moon to our soldiers. Tyrants have never found them apt scholars at geography. They prefer to make their own maps even though they have no paint to color them with except the red blood in their veins. The Kaiser may roll up his War Map of Europe; our soldiers have no use for it, and will not commit to memory its new boundaries. They feel in their souls the capacity to make a new one more in line with their ideas of fair play.

"Eton boys never duck." If the muscles of their necks show a tendency to relax they call to mind how inflexible their fathers have stood in bygone days, and their necks become stiff and taut once more. Wellington said that Waterloo was won on the playing fields of Eton. It is still true that "Eton boys never duck" to the foe; nor do the soldiers they lead.

XI
"MISSING"

The word "Missing" has come to exercise an even more terrible power over the human heart than the word "Death." The latter kills the heart's joy and hope with a sharp clean cut, but "Missing" is a clumsy stroke from the executioner's axe. In a few cases the wounded victim is spared and allowed to recover, but in the majority of cases there is no reprieve and a second blow is struck after a period of suspense and suffering. A chaplain dreads the word. As he opens his correspondence after a battle, it fixes him as the glittering eye of the Ancient Mariner fastened the wedding guest. It leaps from the page at him with the malignant suddenness of a serpent. Wounds and death he can explain to relatives, but "missing" is beyond explanation. No one who has not been at the Front can conceive how a lad can disappear and no one see what becomes him. A man may read graphic accounts of conditions of life in the battle-line, but it is beyond his imagination to visualize it with any real approach to truth.

After the first day of the Somme Campaign we had hundreds of casualties and most of them were classed as "Missing." The soldiers went "over the top" and did not return, and no one knew why. They were simply "missing." Why did no one know their fate? It came about in this way. The men scrambled over the parapet and, forming in line, charged across No Man's Land in extended order. Some fell immediately. The wounded among them got back to the dressing station, and the bodies of the dead were found within a few days, at least. So far, there are no "Missing." The rest of the men press on, some falling at every step; the line thins, and the men get separated. When a man falls his neighbor cannot stay with him. He must press on to the objective, otherwise, if the unwounded stayed to succor the wounded, there would be none to continue the attack; and under the hail of shells and bullets sweeping the open ground, everyone would perish. The only way to succor the wounded is to press on, capture the enemy trench, and stop the rifle and machine-gun fire. Consequently, the man who presses on does not, as a rule, know whether his comrade fell dead, was wounded, or merely took cover in a shell hole. And even though he were to know, he may be killed himself later, and his knowledge die with him.

If the attack succeeds, and the German trench is held by us, No Man's Land can be searched. The wounded and dead are found, and but few are reported "missing." But if the attack fail, and the regiment has to retire to its own line, it becomes impossible for us to search that part of No Man's

Land, adjoining the German trench (for there is rarely any truce after a battle in this war), and so, it is impossible to find out whether those who have failed to return were killed, wounded, or taken prisoners. The comrades who saw them fall are probably killed, for the return is as fatal as the attack. If they come back wounded they are taken straight to the hospitals and so have no chance of reporting to their officers the fate of those whom they saw fall. Only the unwounded return to the regiment and, in a lost battle, these are few and know but little of what happened to those around them. They were excited and were fighting for their lives. They had no leisure to observe the fate of others.

On one occasion our men took some German trenches opposite them and held them for some hours by desperate fighting, but before dusk had to retire. Many were left dead or wounded in the captured trenches, and many fell on the return journey. The few who got back to us unwounded could give very little information about individuals who were missing. They had been separated one from another and fighting hour after hour with desperation. All therefore who did not return to the regiment or dressing station, and whose bodies were not recovered, were reported as "Missing" unless declared dead by reliable eye-witnesses. The evidence of eye-witnesses must be carefully examined before a regiment dare report a soldier dead on the strength of it. During an attack a man is in an abnormal state of excitement and the observations of his senses are not entirely reliable. Men imagine they see things, and frequently make mistakes in identity. I have known many cases in which a man has sworn that he saw another being carried to the dressing station, yet the missing man's body has afterwards been found near the German lines. The eye-witness simply mistook one man for another. No end of pain to relatives has been caused by these mistakes and a regiment rightly declines on such evidence to report a soldier as killed.

Some weeks after the attack just referred to, we received letters from some of the officers and men who had been taken prisoners; information about others came through The Geneva Red Cross Society. Those of whom we heard nothing for six months we knew to be, in all probability, dead. Nine months later, the Germans retired from the position, and many of our dead were found still lying out in No Man's Land. Some were identified. Others could not be, their discs having perished by reason of the long exposure. Many of the dead had been left in the German trenches. These had been buried by the enemy and he had left no crosses to mark the graves. After more than a year there is no direct evidence of the death of many who fought on that day. They are "Missing," and we can only conclude that they were killed.

In other cases, men are reported missing for several weeks, and then reported dead. A typical case may be cited to show how it comes about. We attacked one morning at dawn. The enemy were on the run, and in a state of exhaustion. An immediate attack would, it was believed, carry the position without much loss of life, even though our big guns had not had time to come up in support. Unfortunately the Germans were, unknown to us, reinforced during the night. Their new troops met our men with a hail of rifle and machine-gun fire, and the regiment was ordered to retire. Several failed to return. We knew that some of the men had been forced to surrender, especially the wounded. Others had been killed. Those who returned unwounded were not able, however, to give us the names of those who had been killed or of those who had been taken prisoners. The attack had been made in the half-light of dawn so that our men could not be seen distinctly. They had also advanced in extended order so as to avoid making themselves an easy target. The half-light and the distance of one man from another made it difficult, therefore, for anyone to see either who fell or why they fell. Most of those who were killed or taken prisoners were therefore reported as "missing."

A few days later the whole Division was moved to another part of the Front. A fresh regiment took our place, and, a few weeks later, with adequate artillery support, carried the German trenches. After the battle, burial parties were sent out by the regiment to bury both its own dead and ours who had been left in the German half of No Man's Land. Each grave was marked with the soldier's name, and his disc and paybook were sent to our regiment as proof of his death. The War Office was then informed that such and such a man "previously reported missing, is now reported killed."

There are, however, cases of missing men which cannot be explained. The facts never come to light, and we can only guess what happened. They may have been buried by the enemy, or they may have been buried in the dark by some regimental burial party which could not find their discs. They may even have been buried by a shell or blown to fragments by a direct hit. We have no evidence.

After the attack on Gommécourt a youth I knew had his wound dressed at the Regimental Aid post and was seen, by more than one of his chums, passing down the communication trench to the Advanced Dressing Station where I happened to be. Yet he never arrived, slight though his wound was. It was impossible for him to have got lost. His brother and I made every possible enquiry about him, but nothing ever came to light, and we both came to the conclusion that on his way down the trench he had been buried by a shell. In another case an officer was wounded and four stretcher bearers went out to bring him in. None were ever seen again, and later, when we came into possession of the ground, the body of none of them were found. It was scarcely possible for them to have been taken prisoners, and they were never reported as having been captured. We concluded, therefore, that a shell had both killed and buried them.

One day a rifleman reported sick to the Doctor and was sent down the line to the Dressing Station whence he would be sent on to a Rest Camp. He was not seriously ill, and needed no escort. It was impossible for him to have wandered into the German lines, yet he never reported at the Dressing Station or anywhere else. Loss of memory is very rare, but even if that had happened to him, he could not have wandered about behind our lines without being found and arrested. No report of his burial ever reached us and we were led to the conclusion that he was killed by a shell on the way down, and in such a way that all means of identification were lost. In another case a private, wounded in the arm, was sent down the line in company with a party of stretcher bearers who were carrying a "lying case." Evidently he got separated from them in the dark, and was hit by a shell, for he never reached any dressing station, and his fate was never known.

Conditions at the front are such that these mysterious disappearances must inevitably occur. Every possible arrangement which circumstances will allow is made to prevent them; but they cannot be altogether eliminated. People at home may sometimes think that more might have been done, but it is because they have no conception of the amazing conditions under which the war is carried on. Every officer and private knows that he may disappear without leaving a trace. That being so, they, if only from common prudence and the instinct of self-preservation, combine to reduce the danger to its lowest limits; but, when all has been done, war is war; and nothing can rob it of its horrors.

Every day, officers and men die in trying to save their comrades, and nothing could be more unjust than to blame those who survive for not having done more to prevent others from being lost; for those who are surviving, to-day, may become missing to-morrow, and leave no trace behind. Officers have sometimes shown me letters from poor distracted relatives which could never have been written if they could have imagined the deadly peril in which the officers stood and the manifold distractions that wore them down. Sometimes an officer's letter is short and business-like in reply to an enquiry, but it must be remembered that his first duty is to the living. He must hold the line and save his men; and he has, despite the tragedy of his position, to answer not one enquiry but scores. And before he has finished answering all the enquiries, his own parents, perhaps, will be making enquiries about his own fate. Our officers are the bravest and kindest-hearted men that ever had the lives of others in their keeping; and when the chaplain asks them for details about any missing or slain soldier, they will go to endless trouble for him. They know what their own death will mean to their parents; and the knowledge makes their hearts go out in sympathy to the parents of their men, and it makes them do all that is possible to prevent lives being lost.

When Moses died no man knew the place of his burial. It has not been found to this day. We know nothing of his last thoughts or of the manner of his death. His end is a perfect mystery. But we know that he died in the presence of God; that God strengthened him in the dread hour; and that with His own fingers He closed the lids over the prophet's brave, tender eyes. God buried Moses in a grave dug by His own hands and He will know where to find the poor worn-out body of the great patriot at the resurrection of the just. And God was with every one of our missing lads to the last, and He knows the narrow bed in which each lies sleeping. The grave may have no cross above it, but it will often know the tread of an angel's feet as he comes to plant poppies, primroses and daffodils above the resting-place of the brave.

XII
"IT MUST BE SUNDAY"

The Psalmist of Israel tells us that God has "ordained" the moon and the stars. These "flaming fires" are "ministers of His that do His pleasure." Nor are they the only ones chosen from Nature. Mungo Park, having laid down in the desert to die, notices beside him a tiny flower, and it awakens hope in him. The winter of his despair is ended. He rises again, and pushes on until he finds a human habitation where he is cared for by native women as though he were their brother. The little flower had been "ordained" to minister hope to a lost and despairing traveler.

At the Front such ministering by Nature is of common occurrence. No Man's Land is desolate enough to look upon, but there is life there, and music. Larks have chosen it for their nests, and amid its desolation they rear their young. Even the pheasants have taken to some parts of it. If we could but know the thoughts of the wounded who have lain out there waiting for death, we should find that the moon and the stars, the birds and the field mice, had not allowed them die without some comforting of the spirit.

One Sunday our regiment was resting in reserve trenches after a period in the firing line. It was a beautiful evening, and as the sun sank westward I administered the Sacrament of the Lord's Supper. The day was far spent but, as the bread was broken, there came to us a vision of the Face which the two disciples saw on another such evening in the far-off village of Emmaus. On the way back to my billet I met a platoon of Royal Engineers returning from the baths. One of them had been a member of my church in London, and he dropped out to talk with me. Those who have not been in the Expeditionary Force can hardly understand the pleasure a man feels when he meets someone he knew in the days of peace, or even someone who knows the street or town out of which he came. He was full of talk, and as I listened his excitement and pleasure bubbled over like a spring.

"Last night," he said, "was the night of my life. I never expected to see daylight again. Talk about a 'tight corner,' there was never one to match it, and as you know, my chums and I have been in many. The Huns simply plastered us with shells. The bombardment was terrific. It was like being in a hailstorm and we expected every moment to be our last.

"You know the trench which the infantry took yesterday? Well, we were there. We went up at dark to fix barbed wire in front of it ready for the counter-attack. We were out in No Man's Land for about two hours, working as swiftly and silently as we could. Whenever the enemy sent his lights up, we laid down, and so far we had escaped notice and were congratulating ourselves that the work was nearly done, and that our skins were still whole. Then, somehow, the Germans spotted us, and let fly. It was like hell let loose. We ran to the trench for shelter, but it seemed as if nothing could save us from such a deluge of shells. It was just like being naked in a driving snow-storm. We felt as if there was no trench at all, and as if the gunners could see us in the dark. After that experience I can pity a hare with a pack of hounds after it. But we just sat tight with such cover as we had and made the best of it. There was nothing else to do. If we were to be killed, we should be killed. Nothing that we could do would have made any difference. Yet, though there didn't seem shelter for even a mouse, only one of us was hit, and that was the sergeant. He was rather badly 'done in,' and we could only save his life by getting him quickly to the dressing station.

"HE WAS RATHER BADLY DONE IN"
Drawn by F. Matahia for The Sphere, London

"I am one of the taller and stronger men of my platoon so, of course, I volunteered as a stretcher-bearer. There was no communication trench, so we had no choice but to lift him up and make a dash across the open. They were shelling us like blazes, but we dare not delay because, if we were overtaken by daylight, it would be impossible to get him away till the next night, and by that time he would be dead. So we decided to try our luck. We had just lifted him up when a shell burst right on top of us, and knocked us all down. For a minute or two I was unconscious, and when I came round I thought I must surely be wounded, so I ran my fingers over my body but found neither blood nor a rent in my clothes. I was covered with chalk but that didn't matter. Except for a touch of concussion in the brain I was none the worse, and soon pulled myself together. The sergeant was a sight! He was half-buried, and we could scarce see him for chalk; but we dug him out and got him on the stretcher again. After that we sat down in the bottom of the trench till the effect of the shock had worn off a bit, for we all felt like rats that had been shaken by a terrier.

"Then, as suddenly as it had started, the shelling stopped. The calm that followed was wonderful. I never felt anything so restful before. It was like the delicious restfulness that, sometimes, immediately follows hours of fever. Then, as if to make it perfect, a lark rose out of No Man's Land and began to sing. The effect on us was magical. It was the sweetest music I have ever heard, and I shall remember it to my dying day. The countryside was dark and silent, and, as I listened to the lark, old days came back to mind. You remember that Saturday midnight in the June before the war when you took us into Epping Forest to see the dawn break over it? Well, as I listened to the lark, I was back there in the forest. Then some impulse seized me and, hardly knowing what I did, I cried aloud, 'Why bless me, it must be Sunday,' and so it was, although I had forgotten.

"Then we jumped up for we saw that the dawn was breaking and, lifting the sergeant out of the trench, we rushed across the open ground in the direction of the dressing station. Talk about 'feeling protected!' Why, I felt that God was all around us--that no harm could touch us. A great calm stole over me, and I felt utterly devoid of fear. We had, as you know, to bring the sergeant some two miles to the dressing station, just down the road there, but we got him safely in, and I think he will get better."

While we were talking, a shell burst near the trench where my men had been taking of the Sacrament, and another burst by the roadside close to the Engineers. With a laugh and a hearty "Good-night" he shook hands, saluted, and ran on to rejoin his comrades. The shells were part of the game. In London we had been in the same football team. He had kept goal and I had played full back, and he regarded the shells that had fallen as bad shots at goal made by the opposing team. They might have been serious but, as it happened, the ball had each time gone out of play.

I waited a minute or two in the hope of getting a lift. A motor car came along; I stopped it and got in; for at the Front everything is Government property and more or less at one's service. I found myself sitting by the side of a private, who had been wounded in the face and right hand by the shell that had just fallen near the platoon of Engineers.

He had left his horse with a comrade, and was being driven to the Advanced Dressing Station by a driver who, happening to pass at the moment, had kindly offered him a lift. After a little wait at the Dressing Station I got on the front of an ambulance car. There were only two cases inside, and they were being taken to the Main Dressing Station in Arras. One of them had his feet and arms tied to the stretcher, for he was suffering from shell-shock; and three orderlies were in charge of him. The poor fellow laughed and cried alternately and struggled to break loose. "I'm a British soldier," he cried, "and I will not be tied up. I've done my bit, and this is the way you pay me out. I'll not have it." And time and again he struggled desperately to break away.

The orderlies in charge of him were wise and tactful as women. They asked him questions about the fight, and he fought his battle over again. They praised his regiment and told him it had done magnificently, and he laughed and chuckled like a young mother, dandling her first baby on her knee. And so, without mishap, we reached the ruined town of Arras where nightly the shells fall among the forsaken houses in which our soldiers are billeted. The wounded private was carried into the hospital, and I walked away to my room in an adjoining street.

So ended the day which, in the hour of dawn, the dark had told the young engineer "must be Sunday."

XIII
OUR TOMMIES NEVER FAIL US

On Easter Monday, in the Battle of Arras, I saw two sights such as I shall never forget. One revealed the kind and forgiving spirit of our men, the other their unflinching courage. After burying three non-commissioned officers who had been killed the day before, I reached the Advanced Dressing Station near which our regiment was "standing to" in a support trench. Other regiments of our Division were carrying out the attack and, with small loss, had taken the enemy lines. The German trenches had been blotted out by our shells but their deep dug-outs, with machine-guns at their mouths, remained untouched, and it was almost impossible for our soldiers to discover them until they got within a few yards of the entrances.

The German commander's idea was to keep his men in the shelter of the dug-outs until our barrage lifted. They were then to rush out with machine-guns and rifles to destroy our men who were following it up. If the idea had been carried out, the German line would have been impregnable for our men would have been mown down like corn before the reaper. It failed because German human nature could not rise to the occasion. The German soldiers had been demoralized by the safety of the dug-outs and by the thunder of our shells above them. They cowered in the dug-outs when they should have rushed out. The critical moment passed, and with its passing our soldiers leapt to the entrances and threw down hand grenades. There was a wild cry of pain and fear from below. Arms went up and the cry of "Kamerad." The surrender was accepted and the beaten soldiers crawled out. From some dug-outs as many as two hundred prisoners were taken. In other parts of the line there was a stiff fight, but, on the whole, our casualties were very light. From my own observation I should say that we took more prisoners than we suffered casualties. Some companies could boast a prisoner for each man engaged in the attack.

The Advanced Dressing Station was at the corner of Cross Roads and the sight around it was wonderful to behold. A crowd of prisoners was assembling ready to be marched to the cages, and wounded officers and men, British and German, were being bandaged. The prisoners were hungry. For some days our artillery had cut off their rations. A platoon of our soldiers came marching by, and, to save time, eating their breakfasts as they passed along. The prisoners looked at them with hungry eyes. Our men saw the look and stopped. Breaking rank for a moment they passed in and out among the prisoners and shared out their rations. "Here, Fritzy, old boy, take this," I heard all around me, and Fritz did not need asking twice.

He took the biscuits and cheese gratefully and eagerly. The look of trouble passed out of his eyes and he felt that he had found friends where he had only expected to find enemies. He began to hope for kindness in his captivity. The scene was one of pure goodwill.

Scarcely ever have I seen a crowd so happy. Our Tommies laughed and cracked jokes which no German could understand, but I heard not a single taunt or bitter word. In fact, Fritz was treated more like a pet than a prisoner. One who had worked in London, and who spoke English, asked me for a cup of tea for a comrade who was slightly wounded, and I got one in the dressing station. The platoon of Tommies re-formed and marched away to the battle and the prisoners were led off to the cages. There were still large numbers of prisoners on the road, and they were moving about without guards. Many of them were being used as stretcher-bearers and they seemed to do their work out of goodwill and not of constraint.

Their assistance was of great help to the wounded. The battle was going well with us. Everyone felt in good heart and kindly disposed. An officer who lay seriously wounded and waiting for a car told me of the splendid work which his regiment had done. His eyes shone with suppressed excitement and pride as he told the story. While he was speaking two soldiers came limping down the road and their appearance was greeted with a burst of laughter. One was English, the other German. Tommy had his arm round the German's neck and was leaning on him while Fritz, with his arm round the lad's waist, helped him along. They came along very slowly for both were wounded, but they laughed and talked together like long-lost brothers. Yet neither could understand a word the other said.

I passed down the road towards the line. Gunners of the Territorials were hurriedly hitching their guns to the horses ready to advance to new positions. In the ruined village a party of engineers was already unloading a wagon of rails with which to build a light railway. I continued along the road towards the next village. It had just fallen into our hands and not one stone was left on another. There were scores of wounded men hobbling back from it and I gave my arm to such as needed it most. A badly wounded Tommy was being brought along on a wheeler by two orderlies and as I helped them through the traffic we heard the heavy rumble of the advancing field-guns.

The road was cleared with the quickness of lightning. Out of the village the batteries burst at a mad gallop and down the road they came at break-neck speed. With the swiftness of a fire engine in a city street the rocking guns swept past. The gunners clung to the ammunition limbers with both hands and the drivers whipped and spurred the excited foam-flecked horses as though they were fiery beings leaping through the air and incapable of fatigue or weakness. Suddenly the drivers raised their whips as a sign to those behind, and the trembling horses and bounding guns came to a dead halt. The leading gun had overturned at a nasty place where the road dipped down into the hollow. The rest of the batteries stood exposed on the crest of the ridge. Before retiring the Germans had felled all the trees that grew by the roadside so that nothing might obstruct their line of vision. Such a catastrophe as this was what the enemy had been hoping for. The sun shone brilliantly, and our batteries were a direct target for the German gunners such as seldom occurs. Our boys were caught like rats in a trap. By the side of the road ran a shallow trench and near us two broad steps into it. We laid the wounded lad in the bottom of the trench and sat down by his side. Shells were falling all around and fountains of dirt and debris rose into the air and, on five or six occasions, covered us with their spray.

I covered the lad's face. He was barely conscious and uttered no word. It seemed as if nothing could live in such a bombardment. A shell burst near, and the cry of dying horses rent the air. The traces were cut and the horses and gun-carriage drawn off the road. Every second I expected to see the horses and drivers in front of me blown into the air and I watched them with fascinated eyes. Not a man stirred. They sat on their horses and gun-carriages as though they were figures in bronze. Not a man sought the trench and not a man relieved the tension by going forward to see what was wrong or to lend a hand. Each knew his place, and if death sought him it would know where to find him. The horses felt that they had brave men on their backs and, in that mysterious way peculiar to horses, caught the spirit of their riders. Every shell covered men and horses with chalk and soil, but they remained an immobile as statuary. It was magnificent and it was war. A driver in the battery beside us got wounded in the leg and hand. He jumped off his horse and came to us to be bandaged. Then he leapt back into the saddle. It seemed an age, but I suppose it was only a few minutes, before the obstruction was removed. The whips flashed in the air and the horses sprang forward. The guns rocked and swayed as they swept past us and within a few minutes they were in their new positions under the hill upon which lay the ruins of Neuville Vitasse.

The shelling ceased as suddenly as it had started and we lifted out our wounded soldier and went in the direction of the dressing station. Some distance up the road my attention was called to one of the drivers whom the artillery had left in the care of some privates. He was living, but his skull was broken, and he would never wake again to consciousness. He was fast "going West." His day was over and his work was done. I got him lifted on to a stretcher and taken to the dressing station so that he might die in peace and be buried in the little soldiers' cemetery behind it.

When I returned in the evening to our billet I told the transport officer of the magnificent bravery of the artillery drivers.

"Any other drivers would behave just as well, if caught in the same trap," he replied.

He spoke the simple truth. They would. Such supreme courage and devotion to duty are common to the army. Their presence among all ranks and in all sections of the army makes the fact the more wonderful. Both officers and men love life, but they love duty more, and commanders in drawing up their plans know that they can rely on their soldiers to carry them out. Our Tommies never fail us whether in France, Mesopotamia, or Palestine. Devotion to duty is inwoven with the fibers of their hearts. They are men who, either in kindness to captives or courage amid disaster and destruction, never fail us.

XIV
THE CROSS AT NEUVE CHAPELLE

The war on the Western Front has been fought in a Roman Catholic country where crucifixes are erected at all the chief cross-roads to remind us that, in every moment of doubt as to the way of life, and on whichever road we finally decide to walk, whether rough or smooth, we shall need the Saviour and His redeeming love. We have seen a cross so often when on the march, or when passing down some trench, that it has become inextricably mixed up with the war. When we think of the great struggle the vision of the cross rises before us, and when we see the cross, we think of processions of wounded men who have been broken to save the world. Whenever we have laid a martyred soldier to rest, we have placed over him, as the comment on his death, a simple white cross bearing his name. We never paint any tribute on it. None is needed, for nothing else could speak so eloquently as a cross--a white cross. White is the sacred color in the army of to-day, and the cross is the sacred form. In after years there will never be any doubt as to where the line of liberty ran that held back the flood and force of German tyranny. From the English Channel to Switzerland it is marked for all time with the crosses on the graves of the British and French soldiers. Whatever may be our views about the erection of crucifixes by the wayside and at the cross-roads, no one can deny that they have had an immense influence for good on our men during the war in France.

The experience of many a gallant soldier is expressed in the following Belgian poem:

"I came to a halt at the bend of the road;

I reached for my ration, and loosened my load;

I came to a halt at the bend of the road.

"O weary the way, Lord; forsaken of Thee,

My spirit is faint--lone, comfortless me;

O weary the way, Lord; forsaken of Thee.

"And the Lord answered, Son, be thy heart lifted up,

I drank, as thou drinkest, of agony's cup;

And the Lord answered, Son, be thy heart lifted up.

"For thee that I loved, I went down to the grave,

Pay thou the like forfeit thy Country to save;

For thee that I loved, I went down to the grave.

"Then I cried, 'I am Thine, Lord; yea, unto this last.'

And I strapped on my knapsack, and onward I passed.

Then I cried, 'I am Thine, Lord; yea, unto this last.'

"Fulfilled is the sacrifice. Lord, is it well?

Be it said--for the dear sake of country he fell.

Fulfilled is the sacrifice. Lord, is it well?"

The Cross has interpreted life to the soldier and has provided him with the only acceptable philosophy of the war. It has taught boys just entering upon life's experience that, out-topping all history and standing out against the background of all human life, is a Cross on which died the Son of God. It has made the hill of Calvary stand out above all other hills in history. Hannibal, Cæsar, Napoleon--these may stand at the foot of the hill, as did the Roman soldiers, but they are made to look mean and insignificant as the Cross rises above them, showing forth the figure of the Son of Man. Against the sky-line of human history the Cross stands clearly, and all else is in shadow. The wayside crosses at the Front and the flashes of roaring guns may not have taught our soldiers much history, but they have taught them the central fact of history; and all else will have to accommodate itself to that, or be disbelieved. The Cross of Christ is the center of the picture for evermore, and the grouping of all other figures must be round it.

To the soldiers it can never again be made a detail in some other picture. Seen also in the light of their personal experience it has taught them that as a cross lies at the basis of the world's life and shows bare at every crisis of national and international life so, at the root of all individual life, is a cross. They have been taught to look for it at every parting of the ways. Suffering to redeem others and make others happy will now be seen as the true aim of life and not the grasping of personal pleasure or profit. They have stood where high explosive shells thresh out the corn from the chaff--the true from the false. They have seen facts in a light that lays things stark and bare; and the cant talked by skeptical armchair-philosophers will move them as little as the chittering of sparrows on the housetops. For three long years our front-line trenches have run through what was once a village called Neuve Chapelle. There is nothing left of it now. But there is something there which is tremendously impressive. It is a crucifix. It stands out above everything, for the land is quite flat around it. The cross is immediately behind our firing trench, and within two or three hundred yards of the German front trench. The figure of Christ is looking across the waste of No Man's Land. Under His right arm and under His left, are British soldiers holding the line. Two dud shells lie at the the foot. One is even touching the wood, but though hundreds of shells must have swept by it, and millions of machine-gun bullets, it remains undamaged. Trenches form a labyrinth all round it. When our men awake and "stand-to" at dawn the first sight they see is the cross; and when at night they lie down in the side of the trench, or turn into their dug-outs, their last sight is the cross. It stands clear in the noon-day sun; and in the moonlight it takes on a solemn grandeur.

I first saw it on a November afternoon when the sun was sinking under heavy banks of cloud, and it bent my mind back to the scene as it must have been on the first Good Friday, when the sun died with its dying Lord, and darkness crept up the hill of Calvary and covered Him with its funeral pall to hide His dying agonies from the curious eyes of unbelieving men. I had had tea in a dug-out, and it was dark when I left. Machine-guns were sweeping No Man's Land to brush back enemies that might be creeping towards us through the long grass; and the air was filled with a million clear, cracking sounds. Star-shells rose and fell and their brilliant lights lit up the silent form on the cross.

For three years, night and day, Christ has been standing there in the midst of our soldiers, with arms outstretched in blessing. They have looked up at Him through the clear starlight of a frosty night; and they have seen His pale face by the silver rays of the moon as she has sailed her course through the heavens. In the gloom of a stormy night they have seen the dark outline, and caught a passing glimpse of Christ's effigy by the flare of the star-shells. What must have been the thoughts of the sentries in the listening posts as all night long they have gazed at the cross; or of the officers as they have passed down the trench to see that all was well; or of some private sleeping in the trench and, being awakened by the cold, taking a few steps to restore blood-circulation? Deep thoughts, I imagine, much too deep for words of theirs or mine.

And when the Battle of Neuve Chapelle was raging and the wounded, whose blood was turning red the grass, looked up at Him, what thoughts must have been theirs then? Did they not feel that He was their big Brother and remember that blood had flowed from Him as from them; that pain had racked Him as it racked them; and that He thought of His mother and of Nazareth as they thought of their mother and the little cottage they were never to see again? When their throats became parched and their lips swollen with thirst did they not remember how He, too, had cried for a drink; and, most of all, did they not call to mind the fact that He might have saved Himself, as they might, if He had cared more for His own happiness than for the world's? As their spirits passed out through the wounds in their bodies would they not ask Him to remember them as their now homeless souls knocked at the gate of His Kingdom? He had stood by them all through the long and bloody battle while hurricanes of shells swept over and around Him. I do not wonder that the men at the Front flock to the Lord's Supper to commemorate His death. They will not go without it. If the Sacrament be not provided, they ask for it. At home there was never such a demand for it as exists at the Front. There is a mystic sympathy between the trench and the Cross, between the soldier and his Saviour.

And yet, to those who willed the war and drank to the day of its coming, even the Cross has no sacredness. It is to them but a tool of war. An officer told me that during the German retreat from the Somme they noticed a peculiar accuracy in the enemy's firing. The shells followed an easily distinguishable course. So many casualties occurred from this accurate shelling that the officers set themselves to discover the cause. They found that the circle of shells had for its center the cross-roads, and that at the cross-roads was a crucifix that stood up clearly as a land-mark. Evidently the crosses were being used to guide the gunners, and was causing the death of our men. But a more remarkable thing came to light. The cross stood close to the road, and when the Germans retired they had sprung a mine at the cross-roads to delay our advance. Everything near had been blown to bits by the explosion except the crucifix which had not a mark upon it. And yet it could not have escaped, except by a miracle. They therefore set themselves to examine the seeming miracle and came across one of the most astounding cases of fiendish cunning. They found that the Germans had made a concrete socket for the crucifix so that they could take it out or put it in at pleasure. Before blowing up the cross-roads they had taken the cross out of its socket and removed it to a safe distance, then, when the mine had exploded, they put the cross back so that it might be a landmark to direct their shooting. And now they were using Christ's instrument of redemption as an instrument for men's destruction.

But our young officers resolved to restore the cross to its work of saving men. They waited till night fell, and then removed the cross to a point a hundred or two yards to the left. When in the morning the German gunners fired their shells their observers found that the shells fell too far wide of the cross and they could make nothing of the mystery. It looked as if someone had been tampering with their guns in the night. To put matters right they altered the position of their guns so that once more the shells made a circle round the cross. And henceforth our soldiers were safe, for the shells fell harmlessly into the outlying fields. Nor was this the only time during their retreat that the Germans put the cross to this base use and were foiled in their knavery.

When a nation scraps the Cross of Christ and turns it into a tool to gain an advantage over its opponents, it becomes superfluous to ask who began the war, and folly to close our eyes to the horrors and depravities which are being reached in the waging of it.

There is a new judgment of the nations now proceeding and who shall predict what shall be? The Cross of Christ is the arbiter, and our attitude towards it decides our fate. I have seen the attitude of our soldiers towards the cross at Neuve Chapelle and towards that for which it stands; and I find more comfort in their reverence for Christ and Christianity than in all their guns and impediments of war.

The Cross of Christ towers above the wrecks of time, and the nations will survive that stand beneath its protecting arms in the trenches of righteousness, liberty and truth.

XV
THE CHILDREN OF OUR DEAD

There are times when we get away from the Front for a rest. We hear no more the sound of the guns, but give ourselves up to the silence and charm of the country. Before going into the Somme fighting we were billeted for ten days in the neighboring village to Cressy; and as the anniversary of the battle came that week the colonel chose the day for a march to the battlefield. The owner of the field, when the old windmill stood, from which King Edward III directed his army, came to meet us and describe the battle. When the war is over he is going to erect a monument on the spot to the memory of the French and British troops who in comradeship have died fighting against the common foe.

They were happy days that we spent around Cressy. The last that some were destined to know this side of the Great Divide. The bedroom next to mine was occupied by two fine young officers of utterly different type. One was a Greek whose father had taken out naturalization papers and loved the country of his adoption with a worshiping passion that would shame many native born. The other was a charming, argumentative, systematic, theological student of Scots parentage. The night before we left, the Greek accidentally broke his mirror and was much upset. It was, he said, a token that Death was about to claim him. The Scot laughed heartily, for he had not a trace of the superstitious in him; or, if he had--which was more than likely--it was kept under by his strong reasoning faculties.

"If you are to be killed," he replied, "I am to be killed too, for I also have broken my mirror."

He spoke the words in jest, or with hardly a discernible undercurrent of seriousness; but they were true words nevertheless. The two bed-mates were killed in the same battle a week or two later. I had tea with them in their dug-out on the eve of the fight. They were to take up their positions in an hour, but the student could not resist having just one more argument. He directed the conversation to the New Theology, and to German philosophers and Biblical scholars. He simply talked me off my feet, for he possessed the most brilliant intellect in the regiment, combined with self-reliance and perfect modesty. Then the conversation turned to the question of taking a tot of rum before going over the parapet. He was a rigid teetotaler, "for," said he, "drink is the ruin of my country." He was opposed to the idea of taking rum to help one's courage or allay his fears. He would not, he said, go under with his eyes bandaged. He would take a good look at Death and dare him to do his worst. He was superb, and Death never felled a manlier man. Browning would have loved him as his own soul for he had Browning's attitude to life exactly, and could have sung with him,

"Fear death? ...

I was ever a fighter, so--one fight more,

The best and the last!

I would hate that death bandaged my eyes, and forbore,

And bade me creep past.

No! let me taste the whole of it, fare like my peers

The heroes of old,

Bear the brunt, in a minute pay glad life's arrears

Of pain, darkness and cold.

For sudden the worst turns best to the brave,

The black minute's at end,

And the elements' rage, the fiend-voices that rave,

Shall dwindle, shall blend,

Shall change, shall become first a peace out of pain,

Then a light...

And with God be the rest!"

He was found with his "body against the wall where the forts of folly fall." His brave, intelligent face was completely blown away. His Greek friend was wounded, and while being dressed in a shell-hole by his servant, was hit again and killed.

Some weeks later all that remained of the regiment was drawn out to a little village some miles from Amiens, and very similar to the one we had occupied near Cressy. We were taken to it in motor-'buses for the men were too exhausted to march, and the days spent there were days of great delight. We had a glorious, crowded-out service on the Sunday. It was both a thanksgiving and a memorial service, and I spoke to the men on "The Passing of the Angels."

"When the music ceased," I said, "and the herald-angels departed, the sky became very empty, cold and gray to the Shepherds; and they said one to another, 'let us now go even unto Bethlehem.' And they went and found out Jesus. If the angels had stayed the shepherds would have stayed with them. The angels had to come to point them to Jesus but, that done, they had to go away to make the shepherds desire Jesus and seek Him. 'When the half-gods go the gods arrive.' The angels had to make room for Jesus and the second best had to yield place to the best. When John the Baptist was killed his disciples went in their sorrow to Jesus; and having lost our noble comrades, we must go to Him also. The best in our friends came from Jesus as the sweet light of the moon comes from the sun; and we must go to the Source. If we find and keep to Jesus, sooner or later we shall find our lost friends again, for 'them also which sleep in Jesus will God bring with him!'"

In some such words I tried to comfort those who had left their comrades behind in the graves on the Somme; for I know how deeply they felt the loss. During the week we had dinner parties, and all kinds of jolly social intercourse. It was amusing to see the delight everyone felt at having a bed to sleep in. "Look Padre, at these white sheets," an officer cried as I passed his window. He was as merry over them as if a rich maiden aunt had remembered him in her will. Some got "leave" home, and were so frankly joyful about it that it made the rest of us both glad and envious. We made up for it somewhat by getting leave to spend an occasional day in Amiens. There I went into the glorious cathedral. Almost the whole of the front was sandbagged, but even thus, it was a "thing of beauty" and has become for me a "joy forever."

Except Rouen Cathedral I have seen nothing to equal it. Notre Dame, with its invisible yet clinging tapestry of history, is more deeply moving. But it is sadder--more sombre. Something of the ugliness and tragedy of by-gone days peep out in it; but Amiens Cathedral is a thing of pure joy and beauty. It suggests fairies, while Notre Dame suggests goblins.

While I was looking at its glorious rose-windows which were casting their rich colors on the pillars, a father and his two children came in. The man and son dipped their fingers in the shell of holy water, crossed their foreheads and breasts with the water, and were passing on; but the little girl who was too short to reach the shell, took hold of her father's arm and pulled him back. She, too, wished to dip her fingers in holy water, and make the sign of the cross over her mind and heart. The father yielded to her importunity and touched her hand with his wet fingers. She made the sacred sign and was satisfied. The father and son had remembered their own needs but forgotten the child's.

After all the tragic happenings on the Somme why should this little incident linger in my memory like a primrose in a crater? Did it not linger *because* of the tragedy of the preceding weeks? I had been living weeks together without seeing a child and after the slaughter of youth which I had witnessed the sight of a child in a cathedral was inexpressibly beautiful. The father's neglect of its finer needs gave me pain. We have lost so many young men, that every child and youth left to us ought to be cared for as the apple of our eye. We have lost more than our young men. We have lost those who would have been their children. The little ones who might have been, have gone to their graves with their fathers.

The old recruiting cry, "the young and single first" was necessary from a military standpoint but, from a merely human point of view, I could never see much justice in it. The young had no responsibility, direct or indirect, for the war. They were given life and yet before they could taste it, they were called upon to die in our behalf. We who are older have tasted of life and love; the residue of our years will be much the same as those that have gone before; there will be little of surprise or newness of experience. Perhaps, too, we have living memorials of ourselves, so that if we die, our personality and name will still live on. Our death will only be partial. While William Pitt lived could it be said that Lord Chatham had died? His body was dead, truly, but his spirit found utterance in the British House of Commons every time his son spoke, and Napoleon felt the strength of his arm as truly did Montcalm on the Heights of Abraham. I should not have mourned the loss of the young Scot and the Greek so much, had they left to the world some image and likeness of themselves. In dying, they gave more than themselves to death;

"Those who would have been

Their sons they gave--their immortality."

After a summer on the Somme, I have come to understand something of how fear of the devouring maw of Time became almost an obsession with Shakespeare. Death had taken from him some of the dearest intimates of his heart, and taken them young. And so, like the sound of a funeral-bell echoing down the lane where lovers walk, there is heard through all his sonnets and poems of love the approaching footsteps of death. Sometimes the footsteps sound faintly, but they are seldom absent. How then would he have felt in a war like this, in which the "young and single" have gone out by the hundred thousand to prematurely die?

Others, however, who have given their lives were married men, and they have left images of themselves in trust to the nation. We know the last thoughts of a dying father. Captain Falcon Scott as he lay dying at the South Pole has expressed them for all time. "Take care of the boy," he said, "there should be good stuff in him." He found comfort in the reflection that he would, though he died, live on in his son; but he was saddened by the thought that the son would have to face the battle of life without a father to back him up. The boy would therefore need special "care."

On the evening of the first battle of the Somme I spoke to a young officer as he lay in a bed at the Field Ambulance. He had lost his right arm and he told me how it had happened. He was charging across No Man's Land when a shell cut it off near the shoulder, and flung it several yards away. As he saw it fall to the ground the sight so overcame him that he cried aloud in distress, "Oh my arm! My beautiful arm." He was still mourning its loss, so, to comfort him, I told him that Nelson lost *his* right arm and won the Battle of Trafalgar after he had lost it. Like Nelson, I told him, he would learn to write with his left hand and still do a man's job. He would not be useless in life as he feared. When the children of our dead soldiers charge across No Man's Land in the battle of life they will think of their lost fathers, and the agonizing cry of the young wounded soldier will rise to their lips, "Oh my arm, my beautiful arm." The State is providing artificial arms for our wounded soldiers. Will it be a right arm to the children of its dead? Will it be a father to the fatherless and a husband to the widow? Unless it is ready for this sacred task, it had no right to ask for and accept the lives of these men.

The State, with the help of the Church, must resolve that no child shall suffer because its father was a hero and patriot. The State must help the child to the shell of holy water without the little one having to pull at its arm to remind it of its duties. If the children of our dead soldiers lack education, food, moral and spiritual guidance, or a proper start in life, no words will be condemnatory enough to adequately describe the nation's crime and ingratitude. They are the sons and daughters of heroes and there "should be good stuff" in them. It is the nation's privilege, as well as its duty, to take the place of their fathers.

A few days later I walked into Arras from the neighboring village. There were guns all along the road, and there was not a house but bore the mark of shells. Some of the civilians had remained, but these were mostly old people who could not settle elsewhere, and who preferred to die at home rather than live in a strange place. One house impressed me greatly. It had been badly damaged but, its garden was untouched and in it were half a dozen rose-trees. It was the beginning of spring, and each tree was covered over with sacking to preserve it from the cold and fragments of shells. The owner did not care sufficiently for his own life to move away, but he cared for the life of his roses. And so, when the summer came there were roses in at least one garden in Arras.

The noise of the guns was terrific and the old man had to live in the cellar, but he found leisure of soul to cultivate his roses. His action was one of the most beautiful things I have seen in the entire war. The children of our homes are more beautiful than Arras roses, and more difficult to rear. May we trust our country not to neglect them? Will she save them from the mark of the shell, and help them to grow up to a full and perfect loveliness? Our dying soldiers have trusted her to do it. From their graves they plead,

"If ye break faith with us who die,

We shall not sleep, though poppies blow

In Flanders fields."

XVI
A FUNERAL UNDER FIRE

It was in a ruined village behind the trenches. A fatigue party had just come out of the line, and was on its way to rest-billets in the next village. The men were tired so they sat down to rest in the deserted street. Suddenly, a scream, as from a disembodied spirit, pierced the air. There was a crash, a cloud of smoke, and five men lay dead on the pavement, and twelve wounded. Next morning I was asked to bury one of the dead. Under a glorious July sky a Roman Catholic chaplain and I cycled between desolate fields into the village. A rifleman guided us down a communication-trench till we came to the cemetery. It was a little field fenced with trees. There we found a Church of England chaplain. He and the Catholic chaplain had two men each to bury.

A burial party was at work on the five graves. It was the fatigue party of the evening before, and the men were preparing the last resting place of those who had died at their side. They worked rapidly, for all the morning the village had been under a bombardment which had not as yet ceased. Before they had finished they were startled by the familiar but fatal scream of a shell and threw themselves on the ground. It burst a short distance away without doing harm, and the soldiers went on with their work, as if nothing had happened. When the graves were ready, two of the bodies were brought out and lowered with ropes. The Church of England chaplain read the burial service over them, and we all stood round as mourners. Two more bodies were brought out and we formed a circle round them while the Roman Catholic chaplain read the burial service of his Church--chiefly, in Latin. There now remained but one, and he, in turn, was quietly lowered into his grave. He was still wearing his boots and uniform and was wrapped around with his blanket.

"No useless coffin enclosed his breast,

Not in sheet or in shroud we wound him;

But he lay like a warrior taking his rest

With his martial cloak around him."

All his comrades who had been with him in the dread hour of death were mourning by his grave, and standing with them were his officer and two chaplains. I read the full service as it is given in our Prayer Book. It was all that one could do for him. The Catholic chaplain had sprinkled consecrated water on the bodies and I sprinkled consecrated soil. Was it not in truth holy soil? Behind me was one long, common grave in which lay buried a hundred and ten French soldiers; "110 Braves" was the inscription the cross bore. In front of me were three rows of graves in which were lying British soldiers. French and British soldiers were mingling their dust. In death, as in life, they were not divided.

I felt led to offer no prayer for the lad at my feet, nor for his dead comrades. He needed no prayer of mine; rather did I need his. He was safe home in port. The storm had spent itself and neither rock, nor fog, nor fire would trouble him again. His living comrades and I were still out in the storm, battling towards the land. He had no need of us, but his parents and comrades had need of him. We were there to pay a tribute to his life and death, to pray for his loved ones, and to learn how frail we are and how dependent upon Him who is beyond the reach of the chances and changes of this mortal life.

I was half way through the recital of the last prayer--"We bless Thy Holy Name for all Thy servants departed this life in Thy faith and fear"--when that fatal, well-known scream, as of a vulture darting down on its prey, again tore the air. The men, as they had been taught, dropped to the ground like stones. My office demanded that I should continue the prayer, and leave with God the decision as to how it should end. There was a crash, and the branches of the trees overhead trembled as some fragments of shell smote them. But there was nothing more. The men rose as quickly as they had fallen, and all were reverently standing to attention before the last words of the prayer found utterance. The graves were filled in and we went our several ways. Next day white crosses were placed over the five mounds, and we bade them a long and last farewell.

XVII
A SOLDIER'S CALVARY

There is one afternoon on the Somme that stands out in my memory like a dark hill when the sun has sunk below the verge and left a lingering bar of red across the sky. It was a Calvary thick with the bodies of our men. I was looking for the Westminsters and they were difficult to find. I passed over one trench and reached another. There I asked the men if they knew where the Westminsters were, and they expressed the opinion that the regiment was in the trench ahead. There was no communication trench so I followed a fatigue-party for some distance which was marching in single file, and carrying hand-grenades to the firing line. They turned to the right and I kept straight on. Every few yards I passed rifles reversed and fastened in the ground by their bayonets. They marked the graves of the dead. A few soldiers, but newly killed, were still lying out.

At last I reached a trench and found in it a number of Westminsters. They were signalers on special duty, and they told me that I had already passed the regiment on my left. The poor fellows were in a sad plight. The weather was cold and they were without shelter. There were German dug-outs but they were partly blown in and full of German dead. The stench that rose from these, and from the shallow graves around, was almost unbearable. Yet there amid falling shells, the lads had to remain day and night. Their rations were brought to them, but as every ounce of food and drop of water, in addition to the letters from home, had to be brought on pack mules through seven or eight miles of field tracks in which the mules struggled on up to the knees in sticky mud and sometimes up to the belly, it was impossible for the regiment to receive anything beyond water and "iron rations," i.e., hard biscuits. Water was so precious that not a drop could be spared to wash faces or clean teeth with, and I always took my own water-bottle and food, to avoid sharing the scanty supplies of the officers. After a little time spent with the signalers I moved up the trench and looked in at the little dug-out of the Colonel commanding. All the officers present, bearded almost beyond recognition, were sitting on the floor. The enemy had left a small red electric light, which added an almost absurd touch of luxury to the miserable place. Farther up the trench I found the Brigade Staff Captain in a similar dug-out and after making inquiries as to the position of the Queen's Westminster Regiment which was my objective, I left to find it; for the sun was already setting. The path was across the open fields, and the saddest I have ever trod. I was alone and had but little idea of location, but it was impossible to miss the path. On the right and left, it was marked at every few steps with dead men. Most of them were still grasping their rifles. They had fallen forward as they rushed over the ground, and their faces--their poor, blackened, lipless faces--were towards the foe. There had, as yet, been no opportunity to bury them for the ground was still being shelled and the burial parties had been all too busily engaged in other parts of the field. I longed to search for their identity discs that I might know who they were and make a note of the names; but I had to leave it to the burial party. I was already feeling sick with the foul smells in the trench and the sights on the way, and lacked the strength to look for the discs around the wrists and necks of the poor, decomposed bodies. It had to be left to men of the burial party whose nerves were somewhat more hardened to the task by other experiences of the kind. It was a new Calvary on which I was standing. These poor bodies miles from home and with no woman's hands to perform the last offices of affection were lying there as the price of the world's freedom.

Would that all who talk glibly of freedom and justice might have seen what I saw on that dreary journey, that they might the better realize the spiritual depths of liberty and righteousness, and the high cost at which they are won for the race. It is fatally easy to persuade ourselves that there is no need for us to tread the bitter path of suffering and death--that we can achieve freedom and justice by being charitable, and by talking amiably to our enemies. We try to believe that they are as anxious to achieve liberty for the world as we are, that they are striving to bind mankind in fetters of iron, only through lack of knowledge as to our intentions. Their hearts and intentions are good but they are misled, and after a little talk with them around a table they would put off their "shining armor" and become angels of light carrying palm branches in place of swords and fetters.

This is a mighty pleasant theory, only it is not true; and we cannot get rid of evil by ignoring it, nor of the devil by buying him a new suit. There are men willing to die to destroy liberty, just as there are others willing to die in its defense. It is not that they do not understand liberty. They *do*, and that is why they wish to destroy it. It is the enemy of their ideal. Whether liberty will survive or not, depends upon whether there are more men inspired to die in defending liberty, than there are willing to die in opposing it. A thing lives while men love it sufficiently well to die for it. We get what we deserve; and readiness to die for it is the price God has put on liberty.

Words are things too cheap to buy it. When someone suggested establishing a new religion to supersede Christianity, Voltaire is reported to have asked if the founder were willing to be crucified for it? Otherwise, it would stand no chance of success. It was a deep criticism, and showed that Voltaire was no fool. Blood is the test, not words. A nation can only achieve liberty when it is determined to be free or die. "Whosoever shall seek to save his life shall lose it." "Never man spake" as Christ spake, but He did not save the world by talking to it, but by dying for it. Outpoured blood, not outpoured words, is the proof of moral convictions and the means of their propaganda; our soldiers may not be learned in some things, but they have learned *that*. They know the cause will win which has most moral power, and that the cause with most moral strength will prove itself to be the one with most martyrs. And the side with most men ready to be martyrs will outstay the other. The spirit of martyrdom, not negotiation, is the path to liberty and peace. You cannot negotiate with a tiger. The dispute is too simple for negotiation. You have to kill the tiger, or yourself be killed.

While I was on leave, a man told me that he had asked some soldiers from the Front why they were fighting, and they could not tell him. Probably. All the deepest things are of life beyond telling. No true man can tell why he loves his wife or children. This trust in words, in being able to "tell why," is truly pathetic. I would not trust a wife's love if she could tell her husband exactly *why* she loved him; nor would I trust our soldiers not to turn tail in battle if they could *tell* just why they are fighting. They cannot *tell*, but with their poor lipless faces turned defiantly against the foe they can *show* why they are fighting. Let those who want to know the soldiers' reason *why* they fight go and see them there on the blasted field of battle, not ask them when they come home on leave. The lips of a soldier perish *first*, as his dead body lies exposed on the battlefield; his rifle he clutches to the last; and it is a lesson terrible enough for even the densest talker to understand.

The dead lads lying out in the open with their rifles pointing towards the enemy voice their reason why loud enough for the deaf to hear and the world to heed. Ideals must be died for if they are to be realized on earth, for they have bitter enemies who stick at nothing. And we have to defend our ideal with our lives or be cravens and let it perish.

History, with unimportant variations, is constantly repeating itself; and in nothing is it so consistent as in the price it puts on liberty. The lease of liberty runs out; the lease has to be renewed, and it is renewed by suffering and martyrdom. The dear dead lads whom I saw on that terrible afternoon were renewing the lease. With their bodies they had marked out a highway over which the peoples of the earth may march to freedom and to justice.

The view, all too common, that our soldiers regard the war as a kind of picnic, and an attack as a sort of rush for the goal in a game of football, is false--false as sin. It is a view blind to the whole psychology of the war, and misses the meaning of our soldiers' gayety as much as it ignores their fear and sorrow. The trenches are a Gethsemane to them and their prayer is,

"Our Father, all things are possible unto Thee: take away this cup from me: nevertheless not what I will, but what Thou wilt."

One day, when I went into a mess-room in which letters were being censored, an officer said to me, "Read this, Padre, there's a reference to you, and a candid expression of a man's attitude towards religion."

I took the letter and it read: "Our chaplain isn't far out when he says, in his book, that though we may speak lightly of the church we don't think or speak lightly of Christ. However careless we may be when we are out of the trenches, when we are in we all pray. There is nothing else we can do."

I have been eighteen months with a fighting regiment on the Front, and I have never spoken to any officer who did not regard it as a mathematical certainty that, unless he happened to fall sick or be transferred--neither of which he expected--he would be either killed or wounded. And I agreed with him without saying it. He does not even hope to escape wounds. They are inevitable if he stays long enough; for one battle follows another and his time comes. He only hopes to escape death and the more ghastly wounds. He hopes the wound when it comes will be a "cushy one." The men take the same view. The period before going into the trenches, or into battle, is to them like the Garden of Gethsemane was to Christ; they are "exceeding sorrowful" and in their presence I have often felt as one who stood "as it were, a stone's throw" from them. They are going out with the expectation of meeting death.

On the 1st of July, 1916, twenty officers in our regiment went over the top. Nineteen were killed or wounded and the one who returned to the regiment was suffering from shell-shock and had to be sent home. Although our losses are much lower now, the officers and men experience the agony and bloody sweat of Gethsemane rather than the pleasure of a picnic in Epping Forest. This explains, too, their gayety. It is the happiness of men who know that they are doing their bit for the world's good, and playing the man, not the cad. The rise of happiness into gayety is the natural reaction from the sorrow and alarm which have been clouding their hearts. In peace time they will never know either the intensity of joy or sorrow they know now. A man never feels so truly humorous as when he is sad. Humor is a kind of inverted sadness. The most exquisite sadness produces the most exquisite humor as the deepest wells give the sweetest, purest and coldest water.

Tears and laughter are never far from one another,

The heart overflows on one side, and then on the other.

Our soldiers' minds are not filled with thoughts of Germans, but with thoughts of the friends they have left behind them. Nor do they often think of killing Germans. They neither think so much of the Germans nor so bitterly of them as do the people at home. The Germans have not the same prominence in the picture. Deeds relieve their emotions in regard to the Germans and leave their hearts open for the things and folk they love.

It is commonly supposed (and this idea is fostered by some war correspondents), that when our men go over the top they are possessed with a mad lust to kill Germans. The ultimate aim of a general planning a battle is to kill Germans no doubt, for that is the only way to achieve victory; and if the Germans do not want to be killed they know what to do. Let them surrender or retire. The private agrees with the general in the necessity for killing Germans, but that is not what he is thinking of when he goes over the top; nor is it what we should be thinking of in his place. He is thinking of the Germans killing him. Life is sweet at nineteen or one-and-twenty. It pleads to be spared a little longer. A lad does not want to die; and as he goes over the parapet he is thinking less of taking German lives than of losing his own. He knows that German heads will not fit English shoulders, and that, however many enemy lives he may take, none of them will restore his own if he loses it, as he is quite likely to do. He is going out to be mutilated or to die. That is his standpoint whatever may be the general's or the war-correspondent's. He goes for his country's sake and the right. It is his duty, and there is an end of it.

Most of the killing in modern war is done by the artillery and machine-guns. Comparatively few men have seen the face of an enemy they know themselves to have killed. A regiment goes out to be shot at, rather than to shoot. Unless this simple fact be grasped, the mentality of the soldier cannot be understood. The lust for killing Germans would never take a man out of his dug-out; but the love of his country and the resolve to do his duty will take him out and lead him over the top. It is what he volunteered for, but it goes hard when the time comes for all that.

The unburied men I saw had, but a short while ago, no idea of becoming soldiers. They were the light of a home and the stay of a business. With that they were content. But the challenge came; and they went out to defend the right against the wrong--the true against the false. They toiled up a new Calvary "with the cross that turns not back," and now they lie buried in a strange land. They have lost all for themselves, but they have gained all for us and for those who will come after us. Yet although they saved others, themselves they could not save.

XVIII
THE HOSPITAL TRAIN

We were carried from our regiments to the hospital in ambulance cars. I, and several others, had trench fever. Some were suffering from gas poisoning. One lovely boy--for he was nothing more--was near to death with "mustard" gas. The doctor at the Dressing Station had opened a vein and bled him of a pint of blood. It was the only hope of saving him. But as the car bumped over the rough roads and the gas in his lungs grew more suffocating he almost despaired of reaching the hospital alive. Others were wounded; and one had appendicitis. After a period in hospital, during which we were honored with a visit by General Byng, it was decided that we should go to the Base. We lay down on stretchers, and orderlies carried us to the waiting cars. At the station we were lifted into the hospital train. The racks had been taken down and stretchers put in their places. These were reserved for the "lying cases." The "sitting cases" occupied the seats-- one to each corner. It was afternoon and as soon as the train began to move tea was served. The train sped on and, about sun-set, a most excellent dinner was provided by the orderlies on board.

It was the time of the new moon. "Keep the window open," said one, "it is unlucky to see the new moon through glass, and we need all the good luck we can get," and he avoided looking through the glass until he had seen the moon through the open window. We chatted, read our magazines, or slept- -just as we felt inclined. The night wore on and at about two o'clock we reached Rouen. Cars rushed us to one of the Red Cross hospitals. A doctor slipped out of bed, examined our cards, decided in which wards we should be put, and orderlies led or carried us thither. A nurse showed each of us to his room. We were got to bed and another nurse brought some tea. Next morning we were examined and put down for removal across the Channel.

The nurses are radiant as sunshine, and diffuse a spirit of merriment throughout the hospital. It was a pure joy to be under their care. At three o'clock the following morning, without previous warning, a nurse came and awakened us. We had half an hour to dress. Another nurse then came round with a dainty breakfast. We were then put into cars and taken to the hospital train. It left as dawn was breaking, and we were on our way to "Blighty." We had a comfortable journey and reached Havre about nine. Orderlies carried us on board ship and we were taken to our cots. Breakfast was served immediately. We felt a huge content; and hoped to be across by night. But the ship remained by the quay all day. In the evening it moved out of the harbor and lay near its mouth. Towards midnight it slipped its anchor and headed for home.

All had received life-belts and a card directing us which boat to make for, should the ship be torpedoed. Mine was "Boat 5, Starboard." My neighbor on the right had been on a torpedoed boat once and had no desire to be on another. The lights of the ship were obscured or put out, and we silently stole over the waters towards the much desired haven. There was no sound but the steady thump of the engines, and we were soon asleep. Shortly after dawn we awoke to find ourselves in Southampton Water. A water-plane drew near, settled like a gull on the water, and then plowed its way through the waves with the speed of a motor-boat.

About nine o'clock we were carried off the boat to the station. Women workers supplied us with telegraph forms, confectionery and cigarettes; orderlies brought us tea. We were then taken to the train. It was even more comfortable than the hospital trains in France; and we had women nurses. On each side of the train, for its full length, were comfortable beds and we were able to sit up or recline at our pleasure. Lunch was served on board, and of a character to tempt the most ailing man. No shortage of food is allowed to obtain on the hospital train. It has the first claim on the food supply and it has the first claim to the railroad. It stops at no station except for its own convenience. Even the King's train stops to let the hospital train pass.

We were under the care of a nurse who had reached middle life. She had been on a torpedoed hospital ship! on one that struck a mine without bursting it; and on another that collided with a destroyer in the dark. She was greatly disappointed at the decision which had removed nurses from the hospital ships because of the danger from submarines. She fully appreciated the chivalry of the men who would not let their women be drowned; but it had robbed the women of a chance of proving their devotion, and she could not see why the men should do all the dying. The women were ready to meet death with the men and as their mates and equals. Their place was with the wounded whatever might befall, and they were ready.

Hospital trains have run daily for three years now, and human nature can get used to anything. We thought, therefore, that the people would have become used to the hospital train. But greater surprise never gladdened a man's heart than the one which awaited us as we steamed out of Southampton. All the women and children by the side of the railway were at their windows or in their gardens, waving their hands to us. And all the way to Manchester the waving of welcoming hands never ceased. At every station the porters doffed their caps to the hospital train as it sped past.

There was not a station large or small that did not greet us with a group of proud smiling faces. Our eyes were glued to the windows all the way. For one day in our lives, at least, we were kings, and our procession through "England's green and pleasant land" was a royal one. We passed through quiet country districts but at every wall or fence there were happy faces. We wondered where they all came from, and how they knew of our coming. There were tiny children sitting on all the railway fences waving hands to us. One little girl of four or five was sitting on the fence by a country station and waving her little hand. We had not seen English children for months and Pope Gregory spoke the truth ages ago when he said that they are "not Angles but Angels." The sight of them after so long an absence was as refreshing to the spirit as the sight of violets and primroses after a long and bitter winter.

At Birmingham the train made its only stop. Men and women of the St. John Ambulance Association boarded the train and supplied us with tea; and, as the train moved out, stood at attention on the platform. At Manchester we received a warm welcome that told us we were in Lancashire. Men and women helped us to the waiting cars and handed cups of tea to us. It was raining of course--being Manchester--but as we passed near a railway arch a waiting crowd rushed out into the rain and startled us with a cry of welcome which was also a cry of pain. Most of the men in the cars were Lancashire lads and in the welcome given them there were tears as well as smiles. Lancashire has a great heart as well as a long head. It suffers with those who suffer and the cry of the heart was heard in the welcome of its voice. There was a welcome too, at the door of the hospital and at the door of each ward. Water was brought to our bedside, and then a tray bearing a well-cooked dinner.

We had reached home.

XIX
AFTER WINTER, SPRING

A man's heart must be dead within him if, under the summer sun, he can look on the desolated ground of the Western battle-front without feeling emotions of joy and hope. In the winter-time the clumps of blasted trees looked like groups of forsaken cripples. Their broken branches stood out against the gray sky in utter nakedness, as if appealing to heaven against the inhumanity of man. In a way, it was more depressing to pass a ruined wood than a destroyed village. Some of the trees had all their limbs shattered; others, thicker than a man's body, were cut clean through the middle; others, again, were torn clean up by the roots and lay sprawling on the ground. It seemed impossible that spring could ever again clothe them in her garments of gladdening green. We imagined the trees would appear amid the sunshine of the summer black, gaunt and irreconcilable; pointing their mangled stumps towards those who had done them such irreparable wrong and, as the wind whistled through them, calling on all decent men to rise up and avenge them of their enemies.

But, suddenly, we found that the reconciling spring was back in the woods exercising all her oldtime witchery. Each broken limb was covered with fresh foliage and each scarred stump put out sprouts of green. The broken but blossoming woods grew into a picture of Hope, infinitely more sublime and touching than the one to which Watts gave the name. It was a picture drawn and colored by the finger of God, and it made the fairest of man's handiwork look weak and incomplete. Uprooted trees lay on the ground in full blossom, and shell-lopped branches again took on the form of beauty. The transformation was wonderful to behold.

And it all happened in a week. When our men went into the trenches the trees were black, bare and bruised, but when they came out of the front line into the support-trenches the wood behind them was a tender green and had grown curved and symmetrical. It seemed as if the fairies of our childhood had returned to the earth and were dwelling in the wood. Although two long-range naval guns lay hidden behind it, which, with deep imprecations opened their terrible mouths to hurl fiery thunderbolts at the enemy, the fairies seemed unafraid and daily continued to weave for the trees beautiful garments of leaf and blossom. I have seen nothing that brought such gladness to both officers and men. A new spirit seemed abroad. We were in a new atmosphere and a new world. The war seemed already won, and the work of renewal and reconstruction begun.

And now the summer had done for the ground what the spring did for the trees. One Sunday, I was to hold a service on ground that was, in the springtime, No Man's Land. Having ample time I left the dusty road and walked across the broken fields through which our front-line trenches had run. There were innumerable shell holes and I had to pick my way with care through the long grass and lingering barbed wire. I had been over the ground on the day following the advance. Then it was a sea of mud, with vast breakwaters of rusty barbed wire. Now, however, Nature's healing hand was at work. Slowly but surely the trenches were falling in, and the shell-holes filling up. The lips of the craters and trenches were red as a maiden's--red with the poppies which come to them. Here and there were large patches of gold and white where unseen hands had sown the mud with dog-daisies. There were other patches all ablaze with the red fire of the poppies, and as the slender plants swayed in the wind, the fire leaped up or died down.

When the war broke out I was in "Poppyland" near Cromer, in East Anglia. There I first heard the tramp of armed men on the way to France, and there first caught the strain of "Tipperary"--the farewell song of the First Seven Divisions--a strain I can never hear now without having to stifle back my tears. As I passed by these patches of blood-red poppies I thought of those old and stirring days at Cromer when we watched a regiment of the original Expeditionary Force singing "Tipperary" as it marched swingingly through the narrow streets. The declaration of war was hourly expected and the pier and some of the Sunday-school rooms were given to the soldiers for billets. By morning every soldier had vanished and we could only guess where, but a remark made by one of them to another lingers still. They were standing apart, and watching the fuss the people were making over the regiment.

"Yes," he said to his comrade, "they think a great deal of the soldiers in time of war, but they don't think much of us in days of peace."

The remark was so true that it cut like a knife and the wound rankles yet. I have often wondered what became of the lad that went out to France to the horrors of war, with such memories of our attitude towards him in the times of peace. I hope he lived long enough to see our repentance. His memory haunted me among the poppies of Beaurains. In the English Poppyland there was nothing to compare with the red-coated army of poppies now occupying our old front line. In these trenches our gallant men had for nearly three years fought and bled, and it seemed as if every drop of blood poured out by them had turned into a glorious and triumphant poppy.

The spring and summer have taught me afresh that there is in our lives a Power that is not ourselves. It is imminent in us and in all things, yet transcends all. "Change and decay in all around we see," and still there is One who changes not; He "*from* everlasting *to* everlasting is God." He is the fountain of eternal life that no drought can touch. He heals the broken tree and the broken heart. He clothes the desolate fields of war with the golden corn of peace, and in the trenches that war has scored across the souls of men, he plants the rich poppies of memory. He drives away the icy oppression of winter with the breath or spring, and in His mercy assuages "the grief that saps the mind for those that here we see no more."

He who turns rain-mists into rainbows and brings out of mud scarlet poppies and white-petaled daisies without a speck of dirt upon them, is at work in human life. Out of mud He has formed the poppy and out of the dust the body of man. Who then can set Him limits when He works in the finer material of man's soul? Eye hath not seen nor heart conceived the beauty that will come forth when His workmanship is complete. "If God so clothe the grass of the field, which to-day is, and to-morrow is cast into the oven, shall He not much more clothe you, O ye of little faith" who were made for immortality? His ways are past finding out, but they are good. He puts out the sun but brings forth millions of stars in its stead. At His call they come flocking forth as doves to their windows. He blinds Milton but brings into his soul a flood of light such as never shone on sea or land, and in its rays he sees Paradise, lost and regained. He shuts Bunyan in a noisome prison, and closes against him the door to his beloved Bedford, but He opens to him a magic window that looks on heaven, and the years pass swiftly as he watches the progress of the pilgrims towards the Celestial City. In the mud that has been stained and even saturated with the life-blood of our soldiers, He has made poppies to spring to loveliness. It is a parable He is speaking to us, that the heart of man may feel and believe that which it is beyond the power of the mind to grasp, or the tongue to explain.

The wounds of France are deep and deadly but they are not self-inflicted and they will heal. She will blossom again with a glory greater and purer than all her former glories. She is even now finding her soul, and revealing a moral beauty and endurance such as few, even of her dearest friends, could have foreseen or foretold. For ashes, God has given her beauty, and it is worth all her suffering. Not Voltaire, but Joan of Arc is her pride to-day. When I was in Rouen I saw the fresh flowers which the people daily place on the spot where she died. France knows where her strength lies. Over Napoleon she has built a magnificent tomb of marble, but in it, she has not placed a single flower. As I walked through it, some time ago, I felt depressed. It made me shiver. It is magnificent, but dead. One of Joan of

Arc's living flowers would be worth the whole pile. It is the most tremendous sermon ever preached on the vanity of military glory and the emptiness of genius when uninspired by moral and spiritual worth. France knows. She gives Joan of Arc a flower, but Napoleon a stone. France was never so great as now, and never of such supreme importance to the world. We could not do without her. On her coins she represents herself as a Sower that goes forth sowing. It is a noble ideal, and truly, where she scatters her seeds of thought the fair flowers of liberty, equality and fraternity spring up as poppies spring, where the blood of our soldiers has watered her fields. France is the fair Sower among the nations, and it will be our eternal glory that when she was suddenly and murderously attacked in her fields by her brutal and envious neighbor--who shamelessly stamps a bird of prey on his coins for *his* symbol, and a skull and cross-bones on his soldiers' headgear as the expression of his ambition--England came to her rescue, and not in vain. The German sword has gone deeply into the heart of France, but it will leave not a festering wound but a well of water at which mankind will drink and be refreshed. Wound the earth, and there springs forth water; wound France and there springs forth inspiration. Trample France in the mud, and she comes forth pure again, passionate and free as a poppy blown by the summer wind.

*　　*　　*　　*　　*　　*　　*　　*

9 789357 960953